# GOD AND GOODNESS

# God and Goodness

HUGH RICE

# OXFORD

UNIVERSITY PRESS

Great Clarendon Street, Oxford OX2 6DP

Oxford University Press is a department of the University of Oxford
It furthers the University's objective of excellence in research, scholarship,
and education by publishing worldwide in

Oxford New York

Athens Auckland Bangkok Bogotá Buenos Aires Calcutta
Cape Town Chennai Dar es Salaam Delhi Florence Hong Kong Istanbul
Karachi Kuala Lumpur Madrid Melbourne Mexico City Mumbai
Nairobi Paris São Paulo Singapore Taipei Tokyo Toronto Warsaw

with associated companies in Berlin Ibadan

Oxford is a registered trade mark of Oxford University Press
in the UK and in certain other countries

Published in the United States
by Oxford University Press Inc., New York

British Library Cataloguing in Publication Data

Data available

Library of Congress Cataloging in Publication Data
Rice, David Hugh
God and Goodness / Hugh Rice.
Includes bibliographical references and index.
1. God—Proof, Moral. 2. God—Goodness. I. Title.
BT137.R53 2000 212—dc21 99–053005
ISBN 0–19–825028–2

1 3 5 7 9 10 8 6 4 2

Typeset by Invisible Ink
Printed in Great Britain
on acid-free paper by
Biddles Ltd.
Guildford & King's Lynn

*For Trude*

# PREFACE

THE AIM OF THIS BOOK is to argue for the rationality of a belief in God conceived in a certain way—an *abstract* way. I argue for two main theses. The first is that it is rational to believe that the world exists because it is good that a world such as this should exist. The second is that we should identify the basic fact that a thing is good with God's willing that there should be such a thing. More specifically I argue that we should *understand* God's willing that something should be so as its being good that that something should be so. This forms the key element in the abstract conception of God which I develop. It has, I claim, one great virtue. It does justice to two elements of our thought which are otherwise difficult to reconcile: the idea that the basic facts about what is good could not have been otherwise, and the idea that God is sovereign.

The idea that the existence of the world can been explained directly in terms of its goodness is certainly not new; it is as old, perhaps, as Plato. It has recently been argued for most explicitly by John Leslie in his *Value and Existence* (Oxford: Blackwell, 1979). My treatment of the idea, however, differs from his in two ways. Firstly my arguments are different; and secondly, and more importantly, I argue that this explanation of the existence of the world should be thought of as *being* an explanation in terms of its creation by God.

My debts to the works of other philosophers are too numerous for me to try to catalogue. Some few will be apparent from references in the course of the book; but I have tried to keep references to a minimum.

I also owe a lot to discussions with others on a range of topics, in particular to Simon Blackburn, David Bostock, Bill Brewer, John Drurie, John Foster, Penelope Mackie, Ralph Walker, Lesley Brown, Robert Frazier, Terry Irwin, John Kenyon, Christopher Kirwan, Carolyn Price, Rowland Stout, Christopher Taylor, Keith Ward; and to Eric Heaton, to whom I am also indebted for his encouraging me to think of writing such a book in the first place.

I would also like to record my gratitude to anonymous readers for Oxford University Press for their helpful and constructive criticisms, without which this would have been an altogether worse book; and to Peter Momtchiloff of Oxford University Press for his help and encouragement.

Finally I should mention that, for the sake of convenience, I have used masculine pronouns throughout when referring to God. I hope that it will be evident that I do not believe that he is male.

*Christ Church, Oxford*                                                    D.H.R.
*June 1999*

# CONTENTS

Introduction     1

1   The Scientific Outlook     7

2   Objective Value     16

3   The Possibility of Knowledge of Necessary Truths     37

4   Existence and Goodness     48

5   Goodness and God     64

6   The Problem of Evil     90

7   Miracles     115

8   The Importance of Rational Belief     128

*Bibliography*     141

*Index*     145

# Introduction

MY MAIN AIM in this book is rather a modest one; it is to argue that a belief in God is reasonable. It is modest in the sense that I shall not argue that it is unreasonable *not* to believe in God. I shall not argue that there is something wrong with someone who does not believe in God; rather, more defensively, I shall argue that there is nothing wrong with someone who does—that such a belief is intellectually respectable. My aim is also limited. Naturally I shall not be arguing that *any* old belief in God is reasonable; but nor will I be arguing for the reasonableness of a belief as detailed as, say, that expressed in the Apostles' creed. What I *shall* be arguing for is the reasonableness of a belief in God conceived in an abstract way, but a belief which, nonetheless, corresponds to the central core of many people's beliefs; something that can be understood in fairly simple terms, whose exposition does not involve the invocation of mystery. Not, indeed, something immune from doubt; but something, at least, whose content is sufficiently clear for one to know what one is doubting; and something that it is *natural* for an ordinary, reasonable person to believe.

'Something that it is natural for an ordinary, reasonable person to believe': what I shall be arguing is that a certain belief in God goes rather naturally with two elements of ordinary thinking. The first element is a scientific outlook. The second is a belief in objective value.

## A Scientific Outlook

It might seem surprising that I should cite a scientific outlook as something that goes towards making a belief in God natural. People

commonly think that there is a contrast between the rationality of
science and the irrationality of religion. Sometimes, of course, the
contrast is drawn by those who would say that religion is none the
worse for that. Why, after all, care so much about rationality? I shall
say a little about this in Chapter 8. But more commonly the supposed
contrast is thought of as discreditable to religion. Science is sober,
sensible, sticks to the facts. Religion is undisciplined, superstitious,
goes in for wild metaphysical claims. That this is quite false is something I shall argue in Chapter 1. Science does not 'stick to the facts';
what people often have in mind when they talk about sticking to the
facts is actually impossible. In fact, someone who has a scientific outlook is committed to three things which are going to play a crucial
role in what follows. The first is a belief in order; the second is a belief
in explanation; and the third is a belief in rationality, a belief that
there are such things as good and bad reasons for beliefs.

### A Belief in Objective Value

I have said that one element of ordinary thinking is a belief in objective value. What I have in mind is this. People ordinarily think that
some things are good, and some bad; that some things are right, and
some wrong. And in thinking this, they do not just have *feelings*, or
*preferences*. They believe that something *is so*. They are committed to
there being facts of the matter; to objectivity. At any rate, that is the
way things seem. In Chapter 2 I shall argue that things are indeed as
they seem; I shall also defend the commitment to objective value. It
is here that the belief in rationality that I have mentioned will have a
role to play; an indirect role, but an important one. The point is this.
For the most part the supposed difficulties about the existence of
objective value would also apply to the existence of objectively good
and bad reasons for beliefs. So, our commitment to the existence of
the latter should make it easier for us to dismiss worries about the
former.

### The Reliability of Beliefs about Goodness

The next crucial move takes place in Chapter 3. The chapter is concerned with the question of how our beliefs in necessary truths can be reasonable. In the course of considering this general question I shall argue that our belief in objective value, that some things are good and others bad, commits us to the view that such beliefs are capable of being *reliable*, at least to some extent. And this belief in reliability, in its turn, commits us to the idea that value can make a difference; that the fact that it would be good that something should be so, for instance, can have a bearing on the ways things are—by having a bearing on what beliefs we form. So objective goodness can explain.

### Objective Goodness, Order, and Explanation

So far we shall have seen what our ordinary thinking commits us to: a belief in order, a belief in explanation, a belief in objective value; and, what is more, objective value which makes a difference. These are brought together in Chapter 4. They are brought together in the idea that objective value is capable of explaining, not just our believing this or that, but the very existence of the order. The natural order exists because it is good that it should do so. This is indeed an idea which goes beyond what ordinary thinking commits us to. But it is, nonetheless, no more than an exploitation of what ordinary thinking provides, a natural extension, a natural continuation. I shall also argue that the explanation of the existence of the world directly in terms of goodness is to be preferred to an account which introduces a mediating God, who creates the world because he perceives that it would be good that such a world should exist; and, further, that it is reasonable to prefer it to an account according to which the existence of the world has no explanation.

## Goodness and God

In Chapter 5 I shall suggest that we can understand the account according to which the world exists just because it is good that it should, as *being* an account according to which it exists because created by God. The suggestion is that we adopt an abstract conception of God, which identifies God's willing that something should be so with its being good that it should be so. This conception, I claim, allows us to reconcile our ideas about the nature of goodness with the idea of the sovereignty of God. And it is, I shall argue, a conception of *God*; for God, so conceived, can be thought of not only as acting, but as reacting to the world; he can be thought of as possessing knowledge; and he can be thought of as loving. I shall also discuss the question of whether he can be thought of as speaking and, in particular, of making promises and issuing commands.

## The Problem of Evil

The belief defended in Chapter 4 is the belief that the world exists because it is good. This raises the question of *how* this could be so, in the light of the fact that it contains so much evil. I shall discuss this problem in Chapter 6.

## Miracles

In Chapter 5 it is argued that, without our going beyond the abstract conception, God can be thought of as being able to react to the world, to act *in* the world. In Chapter 7 I shall ask whether we could have a good reason to suppose that he actually does. I shall argue that, although there may be some reason to think that it would be *good* if he did, it is difficult to see how we could have a good reason for thinking that he *does*, unless, perhaps, we arrive at beliefs about his acting without relying on inference.

## The Importance of Rational Belief

A large part of the point of this book depends on its mattering whether a belief in God is reasonable. But does it matter? I shall argue that, in so far as we are interested in the truth, it does matter. And I shall reject two reasons which might be put forward for thinking that we ought to believe in God, even if it were irrational to do so. Finally I shall raise the question of whether it matters whether we believe in God at all. I shall suggest that it is good if we do; but that what matters most is to know what he wills; that is, to know what is good.

## Life after Death

I have said that I shall be arguing for the reasonableness of something that corresponds to the core of many people's religious beliefs, but I should make one thing clear. Although a core element in many people's beliefs is undoubtedly a belief in an afterlife, I shall not be arguing that *this* belief is reasonable. I shall not indeed be arguing that it is *unreasonable*. The position is, rather, that I do not have anything of value to contribute. The sorts of considerations which, I argue, make it reasonable to believe in God, do not themselves, I think, make it reasonable to belief in an afterlife. I suspect that the most that we can say, if we think along these lines, is that it would be *good* that there should be an afterlife. But we should not conclude from this that there actually *is* such a thing.

# I

# The Scientific Outlook

## The Empiricist Picture

'SCIENCE IS SOBER, sensible, sticks to the facts. Religion is undisciplined, superstitious, goes in for wild metaphysical claims.' What does being sober, sensible, and sticking to the facts amount to? Well, here is a possibility. Suppose we thought of the world as consisting solely of the sorts of things that we can perceive, the sorts of things that are the objects of our senses; and suppose we restricted our beliefs to information that was given to us by our senses. That would seem to have the twin virtues of metaphysical hygiene and epistemological security. Metaphysical hygiene, because the only things admitted would be nice, familiar, unproblematical things; and epistemological security, because, if we stuck to the information given to us by our senses, we could hardly go wrong. Should this be our goal? Well, certainly not *this*. It takes only a moment to see that we shall have to stick our necks out a little further when it comes to forming beliefs, or we shall not survive. We shall need beliefs about what is going on elsewhere and what will happen in the future; and, above all, what will happen *if* . . . Just think of ordinary activities. I believe that the kitchen is through there; that there are taps in the sink; that, if I turn a tap on, water will come out; that, if I turn the cooker on, it will get hot; if I touch the hotplate, I will burn myself. We shall clearly have to admit such beliefs as these; and in so doing we shall lose a little epistemological security. But at least we can comfort ourselves with the thought that the beliefs can be arrived at just by extrapolation from the ordinary perceptual beliefs. They can be checked, if need be, by perception; in principle, anyway—we can touch the hotplate, but we may prefer not to. They do not introduce any meta-physical exotica into our tidy world; or, at least, so it seems. We can also, we may think, keep a tidy distinction between the epistemological security of our basic data, the data our senses provide us with, and the admittedly rather less secure beliefs we form on the basis of these data. Let us call this picture, 'the empiricist picture'.

The empiricist picture is an austere one; but (let us admit it) it has its attractions. Alas, however, a little probing will reveal problems. Just *how* austere a picture it is will become apparent when we consider the commitments of our ordinary scientific outlook. But the problems do not lie wholly in its austerity, in the things it leaves out. Its problems lie in part in the undue optimism with which it regards what it allows in. The fundamental positive idea is that epistemological security is to be had if we confine our beliefs, as far as possible, to what is given in sensation. Now the most obvious thing about the picture that I have presented is that it is perfectly obvious that it is entirely possible to make mistakes about the things we see, feel, hear, and so on; at any rate about the things we *think* we see, feel, hear. The bus looks brown, but is actually green. The pencil between the ends of my crossed fingers seems to flex, but it is actually rigid. The sound seems to be coming from behind me, but is actually coming from in front. There is no security to be had with ordinary things. Of course, those to whom the empiricist picture is attractive have (like everyone else) been well aware of this. So they have tended to take the view that we should look for our initial data elsewhere, somewhere where the vagaries of our senses, and the conditions in which we use them, cannot lead to trouble. They have tended to think that our initial data are to be found, not in the way tables and chairs and such like are, but in the way our *sensations* are—'sense data', as these supposed items have sometimes been called. Unfortunately this manœuvre merely creates a new problem, without solving the problem it was designed to deal with. The new problem is how to bridge the gap between sensations and ordinary physical objects. On the new picture, our basic bits of information do not concern ordinary physical objects—'the external world', they concern sensations; and there is no way of getting from beliefs about sensations to beliefs about tables and chairs by any process of extrapolation, nor is there any simple way of checking any such beliefs. I do not mean that this gap *could not* be bridged. I mean only that it cannot be bridged if we are restricted to the resources allowed by the empiricist picture. Of course, one could always try to *resist* forming beliefs about physical objects. But it would be difficult to regard such an attempt as *sensible*. In any case, there is a deeper problem about the empiricist picture. It is located in the idea that information is *given* to us by our senses. The idea is that information is just *there* to be picked up, to be *peeled off*, as it were, from what we perceive; and that is why we can arrive at beliefs which are immune from mistakes. But the truth of the matter is that *nothing is given*.[1] We arrive at our beliefs by applying our concepts to things; and what we apply, we can always misapply. The possibility of error cannot be ruled out. And it is worth stressing that these are indeed *our* concepts; they represent *our* way of classifying things. That being so, there cannot be any *guarantee* that this way of classifying things bears any useful relation to the way in which the world works.[2] So, quite apart from the fact that we can make mistakes in arriving at our basic beliefs, and quite apart from the fact that there is always room for mistakes when we try to extrapolate, even when we are thinking in the right sort of way about things, there can be no guarantee that we are even thinking in the right sort of way. Naturally we hope we are. Indeed we are confident and, no doubt, properly confident that we are. But that we are is in no sense *given*.[3]

## A Belief in Order

I imagine that it is obvious that the ordinary scientific outlook is more adventurous than the extreme empiricist outlook. It believes,

[1] See Wilfrid Sellars, 'Empiricism and the Philosophy of Mind', in his *Science, Perception and Reality* (London: Routledge & Kegan Paul, 1963).
[2] See Nelson Goodman, *Fact, Fiction and Forecast* (Cambridge, Mass.: Harvard University Press, 1955), ch. 3.
[3] For an extended discussion of the problems connected with this, and possible solutions, see Ralph C. S. Walker, *The Coherence Theory of Truth* (London: Routledge, 1989).

for instance, in the existence of items that are obviously not directly perceivable—things like electrons, for instance. There is no question of arriving at a belief in subatomic particles by mere extrapolation from our perception of macroscopic objects; and no question of checking inferences about them simply by looking at *them*, to see if they are behaving as we predicted. But in fact I do not want to say anything here about the specific content of science, remarkable as it may be. Instead I want to mention a more general commitment of the scientific outlook; a commitment which would exist even if science dealt wholly with macroscopic objects—even if it dealt wholly with objects that are perceivable. In fact this is a commitment which is involved in perfectly ordinary thinking about the world; a commitment which all of us have. But it is also a commitment which displays a much more remarkable lack of metaphysical hygiene than any belief in electrons: I mean a belief in *laws of nature*. Now of course such a belief is so familiar that it might not strike one as in any way suspect or surprising. And indeed it really is not. But from a certain perspective, the empiricist perspective, laws of nature can certainly seem metaphysically suspect. They do not, after all, merely describe the actual behaviour, past, present, and future, of actual items in the world. They have to do with how such items *would* behave in circumstances that will never actually arise, and with how items which will never exist at all *would have* behaved. Facts about what *would have* happened. *Very* strange. At any rate the possibility of laws of nature certainly seemed problematical to David Hume, the great Scottish empiricist. He concluded that the only facts corresponding to the supposed laws of nature were facts about the actual behaviour of actual things, together with our habits of thought.[4] Various things happen; various thoughts occur; various expectations arise. End of story. None of these things are really connected. There is no rhyme or reason; just one thing after another. That is what Hume thought; and from the empiricist perspective it is possible to see why he should have thought it. What facts could there be, except for facts about what actually happens at some time to actual things? What would sustain

---

[4] David Hume, *An Enquiry Concerning Human Understanding* (first published 1748), ed. L. A. Selby-Bigge, 2nd edn. (Oxford: Clarendon Press, 1902), sect. VII.

facts about what *would have* happened? In virtue of what could such facts obtain? Where would they be? How could they be grasped? And so on. But it is not what most of us think. When the dropped book falls to the ground, we do not think that it just happened to fall. We think it fell because of the laws of nature. And, when we expect the book to fall to the ground when dropped, we think it will do so because we believe that its behaviour is governed by laws of nature. At any rate, this is so if we are at all reflective. One might think that this was not so. One might think, as Hume actually did, that all that was necessary was for us to think that this had happened lots of times in the past. But in fact, when we reflect on things, these beliefs about the past are not enough, unless they also suggest to us that there are laws of nature at work. Here is an illustration. Suppose that I am playing a fruit machine. And suppose that I believe that it is a completely random device; that is to say, there are no laws which determine which fruit will appear in which window. And suppose that the first ten times I put my coin in I get an orange on the left. Now, to the extent that I go on believing that it is a purely random device, I should not form *any* expectations about what fruit will appear there next time. Of course I *may* form such an expectation. I may expect it to be an orange next time. And that might be quite rational. But it will only be rational to the extent that I *now* suspect that the device is *not* after all random; that its behaviour is, at least partly, determined by laws. (I suppose I should add that I *might* in fact go on believing it is random, and believe that because there have been ten oranges in a row, next time there will be something other than an orange. But that *would* be irrational. That is the gambler's fallacy.)

So here is one important component of the scientific outlook: a belief in laws which transcend the actual behaviour of things; a belief in order.

## Rationality

That brings me to a further belief that is part of the scientific outlook, part of the ordinary outlook that we have most of the time. We

ordinarily believe that our ways of forming beliefs on the basis of
past experience are *rational*; we ordinarily suppose that the evidence,
at least some of the time, supports our conclusions. Not always, of
course. In the case of the gambler's fallacy, the belief is based on past
experience, but is *irrational*, is *not* supported by the evidence. But this
belief in rationality, like the belief in laws of nature, can again seem,
from the empiricist perspective, to be a belief in something metaphysically suspect. When we believe that this evidence supports this
conclusion, this is certainly not simply a belief about the actual
behaviour of actual items in the world. The *conclusion* may be a belief
of this sort, but the belief that the evidence *supports* the conclusion—
the belief that the conclusion is *rational*—is not. This belief about
rationality is not even a belief in how possible items *would* behave.
Again, one might think otherwise. One might think that the rationality of a way of thinking was just a matter of its being a way of
thinking that usually gives rise to true conclusions, at least when one
starts with true premises. But I do not think that that can be right.
Consider this. The human race has, in the course of its history, had
many beliefs. Many have been irrational, but many have also, surely,
been rational. And of those rational beliefs, though many have been
true (or so we suppose), many will have been false. Rationality is no
guarantee of truth. But what if things have actually been much worse
than we suppose on the falsehood front? What if, unbeknownst to us,
a deceiving God has been manipulating things in such a way that we
have in fact been almost always mistaken in our beliefs—unbeknownst to us, I emphasize? Would that mean that our ways of thinking have been irrational? Surely not, even then. It need only mean
that, though pretty rational, we have been rather unlucky. So
rationality is not essentially a matter of being even usually right. (I
emphasized 'unbeknownst to us', because, if we actually *thought* that
God had been manipulating things in this way, our beliefs would, in
*that* case, *not* be rational.)

I have considered the suggestion that the rationality of a way of
thinking depends on its usually taking one from true premises to
true conclusions because, if one thought that rationality was a matter of how things behave (or would behave), that is an obvious suggestion to make. I have argued that *that* suggestion will not do; but

that leaves it open that some other suggestion might fare better. But what I have said about this suggestion will help one to see why no such suggestion will do. Rationality (at any rate the rational use of evidence) is a matter of doing the best we can with the information that we have available, not of doing the best that is possible from some God's-eye view, from some omniscient perspective. It is a matter of doing our best according to standards that *we* can apply at the time, standards that we can apply on the basis of information available to *us*. So they cannot depend on how things *will*, as a matter of fact, turn out, or how they *would*, as a matter of fact, have turned out.

So here we have, in the belief in rationality, another delinquent belief to add to the belief in laws. Delinquent from the empiricist perspective, that is.

So far, the problem with the belief that some beliefs are rational is just a problem about its metaphysical credentials. It is a belief in a funny sort of fact. But there is also a problem about its epistemological credentials. For how, one might ask, could we *know* that such evidence-based beliefs were reasonable? How could we even have good reason to suppose so? Surely not on the basis of empirical evidence. The very question at issue is the rationality of forming beliefs on the basis of empirical evidence. To argue for such rationality by appealing to empirical evidence would seem to be arguing in a circle. There seems to be something rather perplexing here. That is indeed what David Hume thought; and it is worth noticing the solution he offered.[5] His solution was effectively to deny that past experience provides reasons for beliefs that go beyond it. Of course he did not deny that we do form beliefs on the basis of evidence. Nor did he think that there was anything wrong with doing so. On the contrary, he thought that there would be something wrong with us if we tried to do anything else. 'None but a fool or madman will ever pretend to dispute the authority of experience.'[6] But the wrongness would not consist in our not listening to reason; it would rather be a matter of our trying to resist something that was natural and pretty inevitable, especially where such resistance would be likely to hurt us. Our

---

[5] Hume, *An Enquiry Concerning Human Understanding*, sects. IV and V.
[6] Hume, *An Enquiry Concerning Human Understanding*, sect. IV, pt. II, para. 31.

forming of beliefs on the basis of evidence might be compared, on this view, with a baby's sucking its mother's breast. It is natural for it to do so. There is something wrong with it if it does not. But *reason* does not enter into it.

That is what Hume thought; but it is not what most of us think. We think that our evidence does (usually) support our conclusions. And it is not just a matter of our being *caused* to have the beliefs we have. No. More than that: our evidence provides us with *reasons*. Or so we think. That is the ordinary way of thinking.

A further point: I have said that this belief about rationality is part of our ordinary way of thinking. It is, perhaps, worth adding that it is not an optional extra for those who want to compare the religious outlook unfavourably with the empiricist outlook, or with the scientific outlook, or with any other outlook, for that matter. If they are doing more than expressing a *preference* for the latter over the former, they are, presumably, claiming that their favoured outlook is rational and that the religious outlook is not. Suppose it is the scientific outlook they favour. Then they are committed to the view that what is taken to be scientific evidence really does support scientific conclusions. They are committed to something which, from the empiricist perspective, from the Humean perspective, seems pretty suspect. And, of course, for that very reason there would be something very funny about claiming that there was something particularly rational about the empiricist picture.

**Explanation**

I have been concerned with two things in this chapter. In the first place, I have been concerned with the notions of metaphysical hygiene and epistemological security. I have argued that these standards, at least as conceived in the empiricist picture, cannot be met. They cannot be met even if one adopts the empiricist outlook. Still less can they be met if one adopts the ordinary scientific outlook. So, in so far as religious belief does not meet these standards, it is in good company. In the second place, I have been concerned to point out two key features of the scientific outlook which are going to play a role in what follows: its commitment to order and its commitment to a certain sort rationality. I want now to mention a third key feature of the scientific outlook, which will also have a role to play: its commitment to *explanation*.

Scientists believe in subatomic particles, although they are unobservable. *Why* do they? Nearly all of us believe that the behaviour of books when we drop them is governed by laws of nature. *Why* do we? On the basis of evidence, of course. But *why*? The answer that is generally given, the *right* answer, I think, is this: we believe in these things because they provide an *explanation* of the evidence in question—because they render things intelligible.[7] Scientific theories involving subatomic particles do a pretty good job of explaining an enormous body of observable phenomena. The idea that the behaviour of books when dropped is governed by laws of nature helps to explain the regularity of this behaviour, which would otherwise be a remarkable coincidence. A third key feature, then: a commitment to intelligibility, a commitment to explanation.

[7] See, for instance, G. Harman, 'The Inference to the Best Explanation', *Philosophical Review* 74 (1965), 88–95.

# 2

# Objective Value

SCIENTIFIC THINKING IS one element in ordinary thinking; but, as I have said, it is not the only element. Most people believe that some things are right and others wrong; most people believe that some things are good and others bad. Of course they do not always agree— though there is a fair measure of agreement on some things. You do not often come across people who think that there is nothing bad about pain and distress; you do not often come across people who think that there is nothing wrong with causing unnecessary suffering; you do not even come across many people who think there is nothing good about pleasure and enjoyment—as long as there is nothing wrong with the thing enjoyed. There is, however, an alternative picture, which once again one can find in Hume.[1] One can also find it in much ordinary philosophizing. This is the view that there are in reality *no* truths that this is good and that bad; there are no *facts* about good and bad, no *facts* about right and wrong; the only facts in this vicinity are facts about people's desires and aversions, likes and dislikes, loves and hatreds. But this is not the ordinary view of things. Whatever we may say when we philosophize, our ordinary ways of talking betray us. We would not, most of us, be content to stop saying that it is wrong to torture children and to say instead that we dislike, even detest, such behaviour, as if all that was at stake was something about *us*; as if all that was at stake was what *we* felt about it. I do not mean that we might not be persuaded to talk like this for a time; we might even *think* like this for a time. Though I think it

---

[1] David Hume, *A Treatise of Human Nature* (first published 1739), ed. L. A. Selby-Bigge (Oxford: Clarendon Press, 1888), Bk. III, pt. I.

would be a short time. I mean, rather, that to do so would be to abandon, for the time being, our ordinary modes of thinking.

So, in this connection the first thing I want to say is that it is part of our ordinary thinking to believe in objective value; to believe that there is more here than our subjective attitudes. I shall, however, want to say a bit more; because one might think that one ought to make the effort to *rid* oneself of this way of thinking—that this way of thinking will not bear philosophical scrutiny. And it is crucial to what follows that we should *not* abandon this part of our ordinary thinking. But before I go on to discuss this, I must confess that, according to many philosophers, what I have said with such confidence about our ordinary belief in objective value is wrong. According to them, we do *not* believe in objective value at all. Clearly, before trying to defend the belief that there is objective value, we ought to consider whether we actually have such a belief. This will occupy the next two sections. I shall then return to the question of whether there is such a thing as objective value.

## Belief in Objective Value

Do we believe in objective value? This is, perhaps, a misleading way of asking the question, because it suggests that we are asking whether people would say that there is such a thing as objective value. The crucial question is actually whether people believe such things as that pleasure is good and pain is bad. Or (to put it in a way where the answer is not, 'Of course they do'), when they say such things as, 'Pain is bad,' or, 'One should keep one's promises,' are they saying something that is true or false? Are they expressing a *belief*, or are they expressing some other attitude? Of course, not *all* the things we say express beliefs. If I say 'Yuk!' on tasting some food, I am expressing disgust, not a belief. I am not saying anything about the food; I am just expressing my attitude to it. Nor, by the way, am I saying anything about *myself*; if you think I am pretending, that I'm not really disgusted, it would be quite inappropriate for you to say, 'You're lying.' Now, is it like that with 'Pain is bad' or 'One should keep one's

promises'? Am I just expressing my dislike (or whatever) of pain, my
liking (or whatever) of promise-keeping? That is effectively what
Hume thought.[2] (It is a species of what are commonly called *emotivist*
theories of ethics. Less kindly, such theories have been called *boo-
hooray* theories, because they can be thought of as holding that 'Pain
is bad' means *boo to pain*, and 'One should keep one's promises'
means *hooray for promise-keeping.*)

   But one would *think* that it was obvious that Hume was wrong.
After all, you may express disagreement by saying, 'That's not true;
it is sometimes all right to break promises.' This seems to imply that
we *do* treat such things as true or false. (And notice, by the way, that
it is evident that we do *not* treat them as merely saying something true
or false about the speaker. If that were the way you treated what I
said, you would have said something along the lines of, 'That's not
true; you do not really feel that way.') But perhaps appearances are
misleading. Perhaps the fact that you use the form of words 'That's
not true' just reflects the grammatical form of what I said. You do not
*really* think that I was trying to say something *true*. The grammatical
form, a Humean might suggest, though *usually* used in an attempt to
say something true, is not always; and even when it is not, we can
express disagreement by saying, 'That's not true,' and agreement by
saying, 'That's true.' Indeed, he might go on, there are uncontroversial cases where this happens. Surely instead of saying 'Yuk!' I could
just as well have said, 'That's disgusting,' *to mean exactly the same*:
merely to express my disgust. And, in expressing your disagreement
with me, instead of saying 'Yum!' you could have said, 'No; it's
lovely'; or even, perhaps, 'That's not true; it's lovely.' (The yuk-yum
theory of talk about disgustingness.) I am, in fact, not convinced that
this *is* an uncontroversial case, where a sentence, of a type normally
associated with truth or falsity, on this occasion has no such associ-

---

   [2] 'So that when you pronounce any action or character to be vicious, you mean
nothing, but that from the constitution of your nature you have a feeling or sentiment
of blame from the contemplation of it': Hume, *A Treatise of Human Nature*, Bk. II,
pt. I, sect. I, 469; 'Morality, therefore, is more properly felt than judg'd of': Bk. III, pt.
I, sect. II, 470. The distinction between saying that one has a feeling and expressing it
is clearer, however, in later emotivist writing. See, for instance, A. J. Ayer, *Language,
Truth and Logic*, 2nd edn. (London: Gollancz, 1947), ch. 6.

ation. However, I think it *would* be true to say that, if I say, 'That's disgusting,' I would usually be perfectly happy to say 'Yuk!' instead, or even, 'I hate that,' without feeling that I had lost anything I was trying to get across. The question is whether it is the same with 'Pain is bad' and 'One should keep one's promises.' And surely the answer is, 'No.' If I say that one should keep one's promises, I am trying to do more than express my feelings; more is at stake than that. I will not be content to say instead, 'I am in favour of keeping promises'; at least, not without thinking that I have retreated from what I meant earlier. So the cases are not parallel.

Is this enough to settle the issue? Unfortunately it is not. The Humean can concede that the cases are different, but can say that the difference lies in the fact that I *care* about my attitude to promises, and indeed about whether others share my attitude; I do not care in the same way about my likes and dislikes of food, nor about whether others share them.[3] It is this *caring* about my attitude that is expressed, in addition to the attitude itself, when I say that one should keep one's promises. Now, there are various technical problems which the Humean still has to solve, in order to make good the claim that it is possible to interpret our talk of this sort in terms of the expression of attitudes, and attitudes to attitudes. For instance, he will need to give an account of what is meant by, 'If one should keep one's promises, the government has done something wrong'; where it is evident that the speaker is not expressing any attitude he actually *has* to the keeping of promises.[4] But suppose that these technical problems are soluble. Does that mean that he is right? No, it does not. At the moment we have a theory about how our talk *might* be interpreted. But there does seem to be some rather strong evidence that this is not the *right* interpretation. The evidence consists, for me, in the fact that this does not seem to *me* to be a right account of what *I* mean, what *I* am trying to get at. When I say that one ought (usually) to keep one's promises I am not merely trying to get across my attitudes or my attitudes to attitudes; I am trying to get across their *correctness*.

[3] See Simon Blackburn, *Spreading the Word* (Oxford: Clarendon Press, 1984), 192.
[4] For a subtle and careful treatment of such problems see Blackburn, *Spreading the Word*, ch. 6.

Even that is a bit misleading. I am not really interested in my attitudes at all. What I am interested in is what (so I believe) makes the attitudes correct. I am not specially interested in the fact that I favour promise-keeping, nor that I favour the favouring of this by others. I *am* interested in what (so I believe) makes these attitudes correct, namely . . . that one *should* keep one's promises. (What else?) I have this evidence in my case; and I am confident that I am not untypical.

Now, let me concede straight away that this evidence is not irrefutable. We are not infallible judges of the contents of our minds, or of the meaning of what we say. Nonetheless this is some evidence against the Humean. It is some evidence that his account of our meaning is wrong. And so is the actual form of words I use—'Pain is bad,' 'One should keep one's promises'—and the form of words you use to agree or disagree. The question is whether the Humean has any evidence in his favour to beat this evidence against him.

### Evidence for the Humean View

There are two main arguments for the Humean view. The first is that to believe in objective value (to *believe* that pain is bad . . .) would be to believe something false; actually, not just false, but incredible; something so foolish that *no one* (except, perhaps, a philosopher) could believe it. So no one at all sensible believes such a thing. What shall we say to this? I shall discuss the question of whether a belief in objective value is *true* later, and I shall argue that it is. But, even if I am wrong about that, this argument for the Humean view will not do. If the Humean view is correct, I do not indeed have the false belief that there is objective value (that, for instance, pain is bad); at any rate, I do not have this false belief when I am not philosophizing; but I *do* have the false belief that I *believe* that pain is bad. If the argument is simply to be decided on the question of which of these things I am more likely to believe falsely, the answer, surely, is that I am more like to believe falsely that there is objective value, than to believe falsely that I believe such a thing. So this is a poor argument.

The second argument for the Humean view plays a prominent part in Hume's own thinking. His argument is that our beliefs by themselves never have an effect on our actions or passions; they have this effect only when conjoined with a passion (which would include a desire); our so-called *moral* beliefs, on the other hand, can by themselves have such an effect. So our so called moral beliefs are not really *beliefs* at all, but passions.[5]

One could make what is essentially the same point a slightly different way, which makes it look less like a merely psychological claim. One could claim that to 'believe' that one ought to keep one's promises is (at any rate in part) to have some degree of inclination, some tendency, to keep one's promises.[6] To think that it is good to read books (say) is to have some inclination to read books. But that, it is claimed, means that the attitude involved must be one akin to desire rather than belief; the commitment (to choose a neutral term) is to the *doing* or *pursuing* of something rather than to the *truth* of something.

How impressive is this argument? Not very, one might think. One might think that the obvious riposte is that there seems no particular reason why a certain commitment should not simultaneously be to the doing of something and to the truth of something.[7] But, in that case, the fact (supposing it is fact) that to think that reading books is good is to have a commitment to doing something (reading books) need not mean that it is not *also* to have a commitment to the truth of something (that reading books is good). So, one could concede the Humean claim about the commitment involved in believing that reading books is good, without drawing the Humean conclusion that this is not really *believing*. However, there is *something* puzzling about

---

[5] Hume, *A Treatise of Human Nature*, Bk. II, pt. I.

[6] For an extreme version of such a view see R. M. Hare, *Freedom and Reason* (Oxford: Clarendon Press, 1963), ch. 5.

[7] See, for instance, J. McDowell, 'Are Moral Requirements Hypothetical Imperatives?', *Proceedings of the Aristotelian Society*, supp. vol. 52 (1978), 13–29.

this riposte; because one would think that, if it were correct, it ought to be possible to have the one commitment (to truth) without the other. But what would *that* be, if it were not to be believe that it is good to read books without having the inclination to read? And that is exactly what the Humean claims is impossible.

I think that we can throw some light on this question, if we look at two cases of belief which seem to be rather parallel to the belief that it is good to read books; cases where the Humean claim would be at least as plausible. Here is the first case. Suppose that someone thinks that, if all men are mortal and Socrates is a man, it follows that Socrates is mortal. Now, it seems reasonable to claim that he must have *some* inclination to conclude that Socrates is mortal, if he believes that all men are mortal and that Socrates is a man; at least as reasonable as it is to claim, of the person who believes that it is good to read books, that he must have some inclination to read. But surely we do not want to go on to say that this means that one cannot strictly speaking *believe* that, if all men are mortal and Socrates is a man, it follows that Socrates is mortal; on the grounds that to 'believe' such a thing involves a commitment to *concluding* something; and that there is no way of separating the 'belief' into two commitments, one to truth and one to concluding, because the commitment to truth would have to *be* the belief that, if all men are mortal and Socrates is a man, it follows that Socrates is mortal.

Here is the second case. Suppose that someone thinks that all the evidence he possesses strongly supports the conclusion that there is a burglar in the house. Again it seems reasonable to claim that he must have *some* inclination to conclude that there *is* a burglar in the house. But again, surely we do not want to go on to say that he *does not* (strictly speaking) *believe* that the evidence supports the conclusion. What are we to say? The answer, I suggest, is that, in spite of appearances, it *is* possible to think that the evidence supports the conclusion, without having any inclination to draw the conclusion; it is possible, *if one is sufficiently irrational*. And one might in fact *be* sufficiently irrational in the case of the burglar; wishful thinking might get the better of reason. And one might even fail to have any inclination to draw the conclusion in the first case, the conclusion about Socrates, if one were sufficiently irrational—though it would be harder to think of a plausible scenario in the case of moderately rational people. Apply this idea to the case of thinking that it is good to read books. Might it not in fact be quite possible for someone to think this without having any inclination to read, if he were sufficiently irrational? In the parallel cases, he fails to draw the appropriate conclusion; in the present case, he fails to form the appropriate desire.

But if we found someone with no apparent inclination to read a book, would we not conclude that he did really think that this was a good thing to do, in spite of what he might say? Quite possibly. But that is because we are rather uninclined to attribute that degree of irrationality to people.[8] It might be a different matter if *he* found his behaviour odd. The same applies in the parallel cases.

I conclude that we have not found a good enough reason to abandon our commonsense belief that we have *beliefs* that things are good and bad.

## The Existence of Objective Value

There are three central objections to the claim that there is such a thing as objective value. The first is that the supposed facts would be facts of a funny sort; the claim would involve *metaphysical* oddity. The second is that any knowledge we might have of such facts would be knowledge of a funny sort; the claim would involve *epistemological* oddity. The third is that the disagreement between different people, and more particularly different cultures, on questions of value suggest that there are no facts to be had.[9]

---

[8] If one took a Davidsonian line, one might even claim that the principles which govern the ascription of beliefs and desires *forbid* us to attribute such a degree of irrationality to anyone; so that actually, in cases of this sort, the beliefs and the inclinations would be inseparable. See Donald Davidson, 'Radical Interpretation', in his *Inquiries into Truth and Interpretation* (Oxford: Clarendon Press, 1984); first published *Dialectica* 27 (1973), 313–28.

[9] See J. L. Mackie, *Ethics: Inventing Right and Wrong* (Harmondsworth: Penguin, 1977), ch. 1.

### Objective Value: Metaphysical Oddity

Consider a dilemma which quite often confronts me when driving
home in heavy traffic. I have to turn right into a busy road; and in
order to do so I rely on someone's being kind enough to let me in.
Fairly soon after this I come to a junction where cars again rely on
other drivers to let them in. Should I let someone in, performing a
small act of kindness of the sort I myself rely on to make the first
turn? Or should I not, considering that this will, in effect, impose a
second inconvenience on the car behind (not to mention the cars
behind *it*). It is a trivial dilemma, if a common one. However, my
interest in it here is purely metaphysical. Suppose I let the other car
in, and suppose that this was the right thing to do. Now it seems clear
that the rightness of my action will not be just another fact about the
action *parallel* to the fact that it took place in St Aldate's, that the
time was 6 p.m., that there were so many cars on the road at the time,
that these drivers were inconvenienced to this degree, and so on. The
position rather is that the rightness of my action *depends* on facts of
this sort, ordinary facts that in themselves are not facts about rightness or wrongness; that it is in virtue of such ordinary facts as these
that my action is right. No doubt not *all* the ordinary facts are relevant to the rightness or wrongness of the action, but at any rate some
are. Now suppose (what no doubt could not *actually* happen) that
exactly those relevant facts occurred on another occasion, and there
were no other relevant facts. Then it seems clear that on that occasion, too, the letting-in of the car would be right. The alleged metaphysical oddity belongs to this fact: that on an occasion like that it
would be right to let a car in. Now, of course, it is true that when I
have to make my decision I will not be in possession of all the relevant facts; I may not even be able to say exactly what facts would be
relevant. But it seems that, in so far as I think that it *would* be right
to let the car in, I am committed to believing that there *are* such ordinary facts; that *these* facts make the action right; and that (therefore)
on *any* occasion on which such facts obtained (supposing there were
no other relevant facts) it would be right to let a car in. That is to say,

I am committed to a belief in a fact which is, so it is alleged, meta-physically odd.

Why should such a fact seem metaphysically odd? Well it seems that it is not just a very complicated fact about human nature, or the consequences of actions, or the behaviour of cars. On the contrary, it will not even depend on facts such as these. One might think otherwise. One might think, for instance that it must depend on the fact that people get annoyed at being held up in traffic, that streets are crowded, that if people are late, other people get inconvenienced, and so on. That would be a confusion. That these things are so is indeed relevant to the question of whether my action was right or wrong; they are some of the relevant ordinary facts I mentioned. But the fact that, *given these (relevant) facts, it would be right to let a car in*, does not *itself* depend on such facts. That my action was right was due to two facts. The first was that all sorts of ordinary facts obtained (about human nature, cars, and so on)—all the relevant facts that were not in themselves facts about value. The second was that, *when* such facts obtain, it is right to let another car in. *This* is the allegedly odd fact; and, if there is such a fact, it can, of course, hardly be an ordinary sort of fact in the sense of *not* being about value. Let us call such facts *basic facts about value*.

Now the fact that the 'odd' fact would not be an ordinary fact about the world need not in itself be a problem. Many philosophers (even empiricists) have been quite happy to allow facts of a rather different sort, namely *logical truths*, truths that may be thought of as being just a matter of the meanings of the words used to express them. That is to say, they have been prepared to allow truths that are either explicit definitions, or follow from explicit definitions by the laws of logic. So, for instance, they would allow the truth that a bachelor is an unmarried man, on the grounds that this may be regarded simply as defining the word 'bachelor'. They would also allow the truth that a bachelor is unmarried, on the grounds that it follows (rather readily) from the definition by the laws of logic. They might also admit the truth that $2 + 2 = 4$, on the grounds that that could be represented as following from the definitions of '2', '4', and '+'. But, by contrast, it seems pretty clear that it is *not* a mere consequence of the definitions of words, that what makes my action in letting the other car in right does indeed make it right; unless one is actually prepared to count as laws of logic some truths which connect ordinary facts with facts about value. To take a simple example: it is surely not part of the definition of the phrase 'great pain' that it is wrong to cause it in the absence of anything to compensate. One certainly would not have to make a decision about wrongness in order to be able to tell that someone (oneself?) was in great pain. But neither does it seem to be part of the definition of 'wrong' that it is wrong to cause great pain without anything to compensate, in the way in which it is just part of the definition of 'bachelor' that, if someone is an unmarried man, he is a bachelor. Perhaps this is obvious. Perhaps it is not obvious, just because it seems so indisputable that causing unnecessary pain is wrong. But consider a case where there *is* a dispute. Some people think that there is *something* wrong in itself about punishing people for things they have not done. Some people think that there is nothing wrong with this *in itself*, but that it is usually wrong nonetheless because of the bad consequences. The disputants may well be agreed about all the ordinary facts of the case; so *that* is not the source of their disagreement. But their disagreement does not seem to be a matter just of the definition of the word 'wrong'.

So, basic facts about value are, it is alleged, metaphysically odd. And this oddity lies in the fact that they are neither ordinary facts about the world, nor are they logical truths.

## Epistemological Oddity

These same facts, basic facts about value, are alleged also to be epistemologically odd. The grounds are that our beliefs in them are not arrived at in the ways in which our beliefs in ordinary facts are arrived at; that is to say, we do not arrive at them simply by use of our senses, by ordinary perception. Nor do we arrive at them by the sort of inference which appeals to the existence of laws of nature which explain the data we acquire by perception; the reason being that, unlike laws of nature, they do not serve to explain ordinary perceptible facts. Nor do we arrive at them in the way in which can arrive at beliefs in logical truths, which involves simply our (supposed) knowledge of meanings of words together with our powers of logic.

## Disagreements

The third reason for thinking that there are no facts that this is right, that wrong, is the disagreement that is found between people. This person thinks that abortion is always wrong; that person thinks that it is sometimes permissible. This person thinks that it is wrong to eat pork; that person thinks there is nothing wrong with it. This person thinks that it is wrong to eat meat at all; that person does not. This person thinks that there is nothing wrong *in itself* with the punishment of people for things they have not done; that person thinks that there is always something wrong with it, even if on balance it may be the right thing to do. No doubt *some* such differences may be explained by the fact that people have different beliefs about the ordinary facts (including, perhaps, facts about what God has forbidden). But it is not plausible to suppose that *all* such disagreements can be explained like that. It is plausible to suppose that to some extent the disagreements are to be explained by a combination of differences in upbringing, education, and cultural influences and differences in individual characteristics, preferences, and habits of mind. Of course this does not amount to saying that moral beliefs are *wholly* explicable in such terms. And in fact there *are* some areas in which there is a fair measure of agreement. Most people think that there is usually something wrong with killing other people; most people think that there is usually something wrong with causing unnecessary pain; most people think there is something to be said for helping other people, at least for helping friends and relations. But, the thought continues, agreement in these areas can be accounted for in broadly speaking Darwinian terms—communities in which most people do not have beliefs of this sort tend not to survive. Putting these two ideas together we seem to arrive at the conclusion that, since agreement on moral issues can be largely explained by considerations that make no appeal to the existence of moral facts, and disagreement can be explained in terms which make no appeal to moral facts, moral beliefs *in general* can be explained without appeal to moral facts. And if moral beliefs can be explained without any appeal to moral facts, it seems natural to suppose that there *are* no such facts.

### Metaphysical Oddity: Reply

The objection was this. The fact that in such-and-such a situation such-and-such an action is right would not be an ordinary fact about the world; but nor would it be a logical truth. So it would be a funny sort of fact. Basic facts about value are *odd*.

One's initial reaction to this objection might perhaps be, 'Perhaps these facts are not ordinary facts about the world, and are not logical truths, but so what? Why suppose there are just ordinary facts about the world and logical truths?' I think that this is a reasonable reaction. But we do not need to leave it at that.

The first thing we ought to ask is why anyone should think that logical truths are *not* problematical. Well, an empiricist might think this because he might think that there is no problem about *how* such truths come to be true. They come to be true because *we* make definitions; we lay it down that it is to be true that a bachelor is an unmarried man. This seems quite unmysterious. But whether or not this really is unmysterious (or ought to seem so to an empiricist), the most it could account for would be the truth that a bachelor is an unmarried man; it would not in itself account for the truth that a bachelor is unmarried. One might think that there was still no problem. This second fact is just a logical consequence of the first. If a bachelor is an unmarried man, it follows that a bachelor is unmarried. But *here* is a funny fact—that the second fact is a logical consequence of the first. *That* is not an ordinary fact about the world. Nor is it something that *we* make true by definitional fiat. Of course, I do not really mean that logical truths are mysterious; all I mean is that they do not state ordinary facts about the world, nor do *we* make them true by fiat.[10]

Having noticed this, we ought to be rather more open-minded than we might otherwise have been in admitting facts other than ordinary facts about the world and logical truths. But rather than simply saying, 'Why discriminate against basic facts about value?' it is worth reminding ourselves that there appear to be other 'odd' facts. Remember our belief about rationality, which we noticed in the previous chapter, our belief that, in the case of some of the inferences we make, our evidence supports our conclusions, whereas in the case of others it does not. *This* belief was not, I argued, a belief in an ordinary fact about the world. Nor does it seem to be a belief in something which is just a logical truth. It is not simply a consequence of something which we have laid down by definitional fiat that, say, the fact that a coin has come down heads twenty times in succession provides some evidence in favour of the conclusion that the coin is biased, but does *not* provide evidence in favour of the conclusion that it will come down tails next time. That is not to deny that it is, in some sense, a consequence of our decisions (or those of previous language users) that the word 'support' means what it does, and that the words 'evidence in favour of' mean what they do. But that does not mean that it is a consequence of such decisions that this evidence supports that conclusion. It is equally, in some sense, a consequence of the decisions of language users that 'green' means what it does. But that does not mean that the fact that grass is green is a consequence of such decisions.

We might, however, notice that truths about what evidence supports what conclusion do have something in common with logical truths; they are *necessary* truths; things *could not have been otherwise.*

Let us look a little bit more closely at the notion of necessity which is involved here. In one sense of 'necessary' some ordinary facts are necessary. The car from the side road *could not* come into the main road while another car was in the way. It *had* to wait for a gap. But

---

[10] For criticism of the idea that logical truths are created by fiat see W. V. Quine, 'Truth by Convention', in his *The Ways of Paradox* (Cambridge, Mass.: Harvard University Press, 1976), ch. 9.

this is a matter of *physical* necessity. Physical necessity is just a matter of what the laws of nature are. And we can make perfectly good sense of the idea that the laws could have been different. So things could have been otherwise. But there is a type of necessity that is stronger than that of mere physical necessity, a type of necessity which laws of nature lack. Contrast facts about the laws of nature with the fact that 2 + 2 = 4. This fact seems to be a fact that *could not* have been otherwise. Of course, '2 + 2 = 4' might have *meant* something different, and so it might have meant something that was untrue; but that does not mean that 2 + 2 might have been anything other than 4. Well it seems that *some* facts about what evidence supports what conclusions possess this kind of strong necessity. Not perhaps all. Perhaps in some circumstances a certain collection of evidence supports a certain conclusion, but in others it does not—in circumstances where there is other evidence which undermines the first collection of evidence. But at any rate, if we take the totality of evidence on one occasion, and it supports a conclusion, then in all other cases where the totality of the evidence is the same, it would be bound to support the same conclusion. And things could not have been otherwise. It could not have been that this was the totality of the evidence without its supporting that conclusion.

So here we apparently have a type of fact which is not an ordinary fact about the world, nor is it a matter of logical truth. Let us call facts of this type *basic facts about support*. And let us call the strong sort of necessity which they share with logical truth *metaphysical necessity*.

In this company do basic facts about value seem less odd, easier to admit? Well notice that they seem to have something in common with logical truths and basic facts about support. It seems that they too possess the strong sort of necessity, metaphysical necessity. Perhaps this is easier to see if we consider a rather simpler fact than the one in virtue of which my action (in the driving example) was right (if it was right). One might suggest that it is wrong to cause great pain to someone without anyone's being helped thereby. Perhaps nothing as simple as this is true; but let us suppose that it is. And suppose that *this* truth does not depend on any ordinary facts (about human nature and so on). Then, surely, it is a necessary truth. Surely it *could not* have been anything other than wrong to cause great pain without anything to compensate? (You must not reply, 'Perhaps it could have been; perhaps humans might not have been distressed by pain.' Whatever else might be wrong with such a reply, it would mean that you were not, after all, treating it as a *basic* fact that it is wrong to cause great pain to someone without anyone's being helped thereby. If anything, you would be treating it as a basic fact that it is wrong to cause distress . . .) So perhaps, after all, basic facts about value may not be so odd.

## Epistemological Oddity: Reply

It is said that our beliefs in basic facts about value are odd. We do not arrive at them by ordinary perception; we do not arrive at them by the sort of inference which appeals to the existence of laws of nature which explain the data we arrive at by perception; nor do we arrive at them by logical inference from our (supposed) knowledge of the meanings of words. So how *do* we arrive at them? The implication is that we arrive at them in a way which does not have anything to do with the apprehension of *facts*. Is this so?

There are various ways in which we may possibly acquire such beliefs. One possibility, of course, is that we acquire them from other people. But that does not get us very far, because it merely raises the question of how *they* acquired *their* beliefs.

Another possibility is that we acquire them from *God*. I shall leave this on one side for the moment.

Another possibility is that we arrive at *some* beliefs about value in a way somewhat like that in which we acquire ordinary perceptual beliefs, and that we arrive at beliefs in basic facts about value by inference from these. How could this be so? Surely we cannot literally *see* the value in things. Well, let me remind you of what I said in the previous chapter about acquiring beliefs by use of the senses. The senses do not by themselves *give* us any information. We arrive at beliefs by the application of concepts to what we perceive; we classify what we see in various ways. Now it is true that I have said that value belongs to things in virtue of ordinary facts about the situation; but maybe, nonetheless, we can perceive that things are right, wrong, good, bad by applying these concepts directly. Perhaps we do not, in the first instance, *apply* them in virtue of the ordinary facts of the situation. How do we do this? Well, we *learn to do it*, somewhat as we learn to recognize things as red. Perhaps we then arrive at our beliefs in basic facts about value by inference from our beliefs about value in the particular cases; the thought being that the basic facts about value would explain the value in the particular cases. Well, here is a possibility. But in fact I do not think that this can be so; or, at least, it cannot be the whole story. The reason is that, when we 'see' that something is the right thing to do in a particular case, it is not ever (or hardly ever) just a *blank* perception of rightness, without any appreciation of reasons. It may well be that we are unable to spell out the reasons in full; but we will normally be able to say *something* about what sorts of features tell in favour, and what sorts of features tell against. Some indication that this is so is that we would find it not much more difficult to assess a situation that is merely described to us, than to assess one we have actually encountered. Things are quite different with our assessment of the colour of things. And our ability to say something about the features that tell in favour and against does not seem to rely on *inference*. The fact that the action caused great pain (or would cause great pain) seems *self-evidently* a reason for saying it was wrong (or would be wrong).

Is there any other way in which we might arrive at beliefs in basic facts about value? Well, how do we arrive at our beliefs about the laws of logic? Surely a priori, by the use simply of reason. How do we arrive at our beliefs in basic facts about support? Not by ordinary perception, surely. Nor, surely, by inference to something which explains ordinary facts of the sort we know about by perception. It had better *not* be primarily like that; because to arrive at them like that would seem to involve some sort of circularity, as I remarked in the previous chapter. It seems that we would be relying on the fact that evidence of such-and-such a sort supported such-and-such conclusions in arriving at the belief that this was so. In any case, it is not at all clear *what* ordinary facts would be explained by basic facts about support. About the only plausible candidate would be the fact that we have these beliefs about support; but that, of course, would mean that we had acquired the belief by some other means in the first place. It would also not do justice to the fact that it seems *self-evidently* the case that *this* sort of evidence supports *that* sort of conclusion. The obvious answer is that here too we arrive at such beliefs a priori. So what about beliefs in basic facts about value? The obvious answer is that there, too, we arrive at the beliefs a priori. That is just how one would expect to arrive at beliefs in necessary truths.

Actually, we shall see that the question of how knowledge of necessary truths is possible is *not* entirely straightforward—even if we give the method a name: a priori. But this is a general problem for knowledge of necessary truth of all sorts, including logical truth. It is not a problem that is specific to the idea that we arrive at our beliefs in basic facts about value like this. We shall return to this problem in the next chapter.

### Disagreement: Reply

The objection was that disagreement about value, at any rate about *basic* facts about value, could be explained by various facts about us and our environment that had nothing to do with *value*; and that agreement could be explained in Darwinian terms, again without reference to any facts about value. So it seemed that belief in this area in general could be explained without reference to facts about value. And this, it was argued, suggested that there *were* no such facts.

There are a number of things to notice about this argument. The first thing to notice is that it is not as if we actually *have* well-worked-out explanations of the supposed sort, well supported by evidence, for the majority of cases. It is rather that people think they can see how such explanations would work.

The second thing to notice is that, even if there *is* some apprehension of facts about value in some cases, we should *expect* there to be disagreement, and we should expect some of the conflicting beliefs to be partially or wholly explicable in terms that make no mention of value. This is because our beliefs about value generally (even if not always) have a bearing on the way we feel about courses of action and on the way we act. This means that they can come into conflict, directly or indirectly, with desires (our own or others) and interests (our own or others). And this, in its turn, means that there may be pressure (conscious or otherwise) to change our beliefs. So, the fact that we find explanations of this sort in some cases should not lead us to suppose that in no cases is there any apprehension of facts about value. If anything, we should be more worried if we found no such explanations in cases of disagreement. Of course we do not find so much divergence of opinion in the case of beliefs about support, because there is not the same intimate connection between such beliefs and *types* of action. (Though we *do* find wishful thinking occasionally. And we do, notoriously, find divergence of opinion about the strength of arguments for the existence of God.)

The third thing to notice is that it is *not* so obvious that a straight-forward Darwinian account can be given about agreement. It is perfectly true that *if* a society has beliefs about value, and if some of these beliefs have more survival value than others, then we may expect that those with greater survival value will persist, and that those with less survival value will not. It is also quite plausible to suppose that, amongst such beliefs, a belief in the importance of helping other members of one's community is likely to have a good deal of survival value: communities where people tend to cooperate are more likely to survive than those where they do not. What is much *less* obvious is what the survival value is of having beliefs about value *at all*. It would seem that, from the point of view of survival, having cooperative desires in common would do just as well. It works well for other animals. Why not for humans? Why do we not find among humans a broad mixture of people, some of whom have beliefs about values and some of whom do not? Why should adherence to a *false* view be so dominant?

## Is There Objective Value?

We believe in objective value. Should we, in the light of the objections, abandon this belief? Perhaps this is an unrealistic question.

Perhaps it would be more or less impossible to abandon the belief, because it is more or less *impossible* to stop thinking that one should avoid causing unnecessary pain, that it is wrong to torture children (and so on). But should we at least recognize, when we stand back from ourselves, that these beliefs are probably false? Surely we should not.

I have suggested that we should not regard basic facts about value as metaphysically odd. But even if they *do* seem to us a little odd, we should ask ourselves two questions. The first is whether they are so much odder than other facts which we appear to believe in, basic facts about support, and logical truths. And, if they do not seem odder, do we feel strongly inclined to regard these beliefs as false too? There would be a major difficulty. As I mentioned in the previous chapter, to start regarding our beliefs in *this* area as false is going to put pressure on the whole idea that we *should* regard some beliefs as false. But whatever the answer to this question is, we should notice that the worries about the metaphysical credentials of basic facts about value amount, at the very most, to *beliefs* of a certain sort. The second thing, then, which we should ask ourselves, if we have such beliefs, and if they seem to come into conflict with our beliefs about value, is this. Which beliefs should give way? Should we favour our highly abstract metaphysical worries over our apparently firm conviction that it is *wrong* to torture children? One could say something similar about the objection which appeals to epistemological oddity.

But what about the objection based on the possibility of explaining agreement and disagreement without reference to value? It is doubtful whether, *at its best*, the case for the opposition is any stronger than this: the possibility of explaining our beliefs in terms which have no reference to any apprehension of value looks as promising as the possibility of explaining them in terms which *do* make reference to the apprehension of value (and other factors as well, of course). Where does that leave us? I think that if we are impressed by this objection, it is likely to be because we think that, other things being equal, it is better to accept an explanation of a relatively familiar sort, rather than one which refers to something as odd as the apprehension of facts about value. Now, in the first place, this means that a good deal of reliance has to be placed on the first two objections. But, in the second place, it is important to remember that other things are *not* equal. It is not as if we are neutral observers of these people who have these beliefs. It is not as if we are simply to decide between the mere *hypothesis* that there are facts about value which explain these beliefs, and the competing hypothesis that the beliefs are to be explained in Darwinian terms. These beliefs are *our* beliefs. Any sort of predilection which we might have in the abstract for the latter explanation must contend with the predilection which is constituted by our actual beliefs about value. It is my contention that it is these beliefs which win; and it is these beliefs which *should* win.

# 3

# The Possibility of Knowledge
# of Necessary Truths

IN THE LAST CHAPTER I argued that we believe in a variety of necessary truths: logical truths, mathematical truths (if they are different), basic truths about evidential support, basic truths about value. We not only believe many such truths, we also think that our beliefs are reasonable. In some cases we even think we have knowledge. The questions I want to consider in this chapter are, 'How is such knowledge possible?' and, 'How is such reasonable belief possible?' These questions are important for two reasons. The first reason is that, if the answer is that both knowledge and reasonable belief are *impossible* in these areas, we might want to revise our belief that there are any *facts* in these areas. There would be a problem about going on believing in such facts, if we were forced to the conclusion that all such beliefs were unreasonable. Of course, I do not expect to arrive at the conclusion that knowledge and reasonable belief are *not* possible. On the contrary I shall offer an account of how they *are* possible. The second reason is that I shall want to appeal to this account in what follows.

## Why Is There a Problem?

One might think that one could answer the questions just by saying that we can arrive at beliefs in these areas a priori. But that reply, though I think it is perfectly correct, would be superficial. The easiest way to see that there is a real problem is if we consider a plausible account of the nature of knowledge. Not all beliefs, even true beliefs, constitute knowledge. If, for instance, I am right about something by pure luck, my belief will not count as knowledge. For it to count as knowledge, it seems, my belief must have been arrived at in some reliable way, some way that made it likely that my belief would be true. And this seems to require that the way of arriving at the belief should provide for some *connection* between the beliefs to which it gives rise and the facts that are relevant to their truth, or, at the very least, should be capable of giving rise to such a connection. If there were no such connection, and could be no such connection, it is difficult to see how the way of arriving at the beliefs in question could be suitably reliable. But what sort of connection might there be? The most obvious candidate is a causal connection of some sort, direct or indirect; but it is difficult to see how there could be a *causal* connection in the cases we are interested in, where the facts are *necessary* facts. Surely, one might think, necessary facts do not cause anything. And, even if one necessary fact might be thought of as in some sense responsible for another *necessary* fact, it surely could not be responsible for a *contingent* fact (that is, for a non-necessary fact). But, equally, it seems impossible that the required connection could arise from the fact that some third thing should be responsible for both the contingent fact (of our having such-and-such a belief) and the necessary fact we believe in. For the third thing would have to be itself either necessary or contingent. If it were necessary, the problem would arise all over again of how *it* could cause the contingent fact of our belief. But if it were contingent, it is hard to see how it could be responsible for the necessary fact that we believe in.

So there is a problem about how knowledge of necessary truths is possible; at least, if reliability is required for knowledge. But perhaps reliability is not required for knowledge. Or perhaps, even if it is required for *knowledge*, it is not required for reasonable belief; so that, even if there is a problem about knowledge, there is no such problem about reasonable belief. Indeed, it might seem plausible to suggest that what makes a belief reasonable is just the way it relates to other beliefs; there need be no connection with the *facts*.[1] For

---

[1]  See Laurence BonJour, *The Structure of Empirical Knowledge* (Cambridge, Mass.: Harvard University Press, 1985).

instance one might think that the reasonableness of a set of beliefs was a matter of its internal coherence, how the beliefs fit with each other and give each other mutual support. So, if we stick to the question of how reasonable belief is possible, can we sidestep the problems about reliability? The answer is, 'No.' Even if reasonableness does not depend on any relation of the set of beliefs to things outside, that does not mean that we, as would-be reasonable believers, can ignore the question of the relation between our beliefs and other things. The reason is this. It would surely be irrational to combine a belief that something was so, that $2 + 2 = 4$, let us say, with a belief that it is sheer chance if beliefs arrived at in that way are true; it would surely be irrational to combine a belief that $2 + 2 = 4$ with a belief that there is no reason to suppose that beliefs arrived at in that way are likely to be true. Here is an illustration. In the process of subjecting all his former beliefs to doubt, Descartes considers the hypothesis that they were all inserted in him by a *malin génie*, a being of the utmost power and cunning which has employed all his energies in order to deceive him.[2] Well, it would surely be irrational to believe that $2 + 2 = 4$, and at the same time to believe that one had no good reason for thinking that this belief had not been inserted by a *malin génie*. So, even if it is possible to have rational beliefs without their having been reliably arrived at, and even if it is possible to have rational beliefs without having any views about whether they have been reliably arrived at, it seems harder to combine having rational beliefs with *recklessness* about how they have been arrived at. So, why, actually, could we not avoid the problem of reliability on the supposition that the reasonableness of a set of beliefs is just a matter of coherence? The reason is that there is one thing which will certainly put coherence in danger. It will be in danger precisely if one member of the set is the belief that there is no reason to suppose that some other members have been arrived at in a reliable way. The threat will be even greater if it seems that there *could not* be a way in which those members had been reliably arrived at. No doubt one should not

[2] R. Descartes, *Meditations on First Philosophy* (first published 1641) in *The Philosophical Writings of Descartes*, trans. J. Cottingham, R. Stoothoff, and D. Murdoch (Cambridge: Cambridge University Press, 1984), vol. ii, First Meditation.

exaggerate the threat. It could hardly be claimed that all our beliefs
are unreasonable until we have removed it. But we certainly have an
*interest* in removing the threat.

So, there is a problem. Is there a solution?

### A Solution that Appeals to a Coherence Theory of Truth

It might be suggested that the problem arises from looking at things
the wrong way round. It is not that there are facts which are quite
independent of beliefs, so that we then have to worry about whether
our beliefs could be reliably related to these independent facts. On the
contrary, the facts are simply *constituted* by the contents of a suitable
set of beliefs, namely, a coherent set of beliefs. One might go on as
follows. It is coherence indeed which makes beliefs rational; but since
it is the coherence of a set of beliefs which determines what the facts
*are*, this coherence, this rationality, cannot depend on the existence
of a reliable connection between the beliefs and the facts. A theory of
this sort is a *coherence theory of truth*.

So, is this a good solution? Well, it clearly would not be if a coherence theory were not correct, at least about necessary truth. And it is
difficult to see that a coherence theory *could* be right about necessary
truths in general. The reason is this. A coherence theory holds that
truth in a certain area is *constituted* by the contents of a certain set
of coherent beliefs. But what about the fact that the beliefs *are* coherent? *That* can hardly be constituted merely by the *content* of the
beliefs. It must be something over and above what is believed, or there
will be no distinction between true beliefs about coherence and false
beliefs about coherence. So there seem to be some truths to which the
coherence theory of truth does not apply: namely, truths about the
coherence (or lack of coherence) of a given set of beliefs. Well, what
*does* coherence consist in? Now, this is a general problem which a
coherence theory has to face—the problem of specifying what the
coherence it speaks of consists in. The less it includes, the less plausible is the claim that truth is constituted by such coherence. So one
might expect the holding of appropriate logical relations to be a

requirement; also the existence of mutual support. But, at the very least, logical consistency must be a requirement. So, however one looks at it, there are going to be some necessary truths to which the theory does not apply.

But even if a coherence theory *were* correct, it would not solve our problem. The reason is that, on any plausible version of such a theory, truth is constituted, not by any old moderately coherent set of beliefs, but by some *ideal* set—perhaps an ideally coherent improvement on the set in question; because, of course, a moderately coherent set might contain some beliefs which would be abandoned as false by an improved set of beliefs.[3] But in that case the question remains: is there any reason to suppose that there is some reliable connection between our actual beliefs and the relevant ideal set? To which we might add that, even if the coherence theorist were right, and coherence did not depend on the relation of beliefs to facts, it would not follow that the ideal coherence of a set did not involve its containing *beliefs* about the reliable connection between beliefs and facts—and these beliefs about reliable connections would, of course, have to be *rational* beliefs.

## A Solution in Terms of What Constitutes Having the Relevant Beliefs

The previous solution tried to bridge the gap by representing the truth of a set of beliefs as closer than one might think to its reasonableness. The present solution tries to bridge the gap by representing believing as closer than one might think to truth. The sort of solution I have in mind is one which says that we would not *count* as having beliefs of the relevant sort unless they were by and large true. So, beliefs of the relevant sort are *bound* to be arrived at reliably—or pretty reliably.

Perhaps such a solution would have the best chance of success in the case of logical beliefs. A version might go like this.

---

[3] See Blackburn, *Spreading the Word*, ch. 6, sect. 3.

The first claim is that we would not count as having thoughts at all unless our thoughts obeyed the laws of logic, at any rate for the most part. There is a limit to how inconsistent thoughts can be if they are to have any determinate content; and if, so to speak, they had no determinate content, they would not be thoughts. The second claim is that we would not count as having beliefs on logical matters unless they reflected our logical processes. When these two claims are put together, it would seem to follow that we would not count as having beliefs on logical matters unless such beliefs were by and large true.

I will not spend long on this. Even if it were right (which I doubt), it would not solve our problem. Our problem is that it seems difficult to see how we could reasonably believe something, if we think that there is no way in which we could have arrived at the belief which would make it likely that it was true. We had been supposing that there was no problem about how beliefs might arise in themselves; the problem was how they could arise in such a way as to reflect the facts. Now it is being claimed that the states of mind will not be beliefs unless (by and large) they have the appropriate logical relations (reflect the logical facts). So *if* we have beliefs on logical matters, they *will* reflect the facts. But that does not solve the problem. It merely relocates it. The problem now becomes a problem of how states of mind can be brought about in such a way as to reflect the logical facts (and so qualify as beliefs). That is to say, it becomes a problem of how beliefs about logical matters are possible at all, rather than how they could be reliable. But the basic problem of the relation between the mind and the facts remains unsolved.

## A Darwinian Solution

We believe that our ways of arriving at beliefs about necessary truths are reliable. So, we would like an account of how this reliability might have come about. Here is what looks like a promising suggestion. We can account for the reliability without supposing that the facts had any role in giving rise to our ways of arriving at these beliefs. We may suppose, instead, that the ways of arriving at such beliefs arise by chance; as a result of random mutation, perhaps. Nonetheless, so it is suggested, our beliefs are likely to be *right*, because belief-forming methods that give rise to predominantly true beliefs are more likely to be conducive to survival than ones that give rise to predominantly false ones. Reliable belief-forming methods are more likely to be selected than unreliable ones. And our methods have, after all, survived.

Alas, this solution will not work for a quite general reason. The reason is that the *truth* of our beliefs about necessary facts is, in itself, simply *irrelevant* to survival. It may matter that we have reliable methods for beliefs about particular things; but it does not matter in the case of necessary truths.

This is particularly easy to see in the case of moral beliefs. All that matters from the point of view of survival is that such beliefs should be *useful*; that they should yield appropriate behaviour. It would have been all the same from this point of view if all such beliefs had been false—indeed, if there had been no moral facts at all—as long as they led to the behaviour they did. Indeed, it is hardly surprising if a Darwinian solution will not work here, because, as we noticed in the previous chapter, the availability of a Darwinian explanation for our moral beliefs is generally thought be a reason for saying that there are *no* moral facts. But it is worth noticing that the Darwinian solution will not work even in the case of logical truth; for otherwise it might be thought that we have here a reason for accepting that there is such a thing as logical truth, while denying that there are any facts about value.

Let us consider our beliefs in logical truth, then. Take a specific belief. We think that, if anything is sweet and poisonous, it must be poisonous. That is an understatement. It seems impossible that we could be wrong. But if this is more than an illusion, an inescapable illusion perhaps, there must be *something* that has made it likely that this conviction matches the facts. Could it be natural selection? Could it be that we would have been unlikely to have survived if this conviction had not been true? Here are two considerations which each suggest that the answer is, 'No.'

The first consideration is this. Suppose there were no necessary truths at all. That would mean that our conviction that, if anything is sweet and poisonous, it *must* be poisonous would be *false*. But would this falsity have any bearing on our chances of survival? The belief may perhaps have a bearing on what beliefs about particular things we form, and they in turn may be more or less useful. But their usefulness does not in any way depend on the *truth* of the metaphysical belief about necessity which gave rise to them. What bearing would the nonexistence of necessary facts have on the behaviour of particular things? It is, of course, precisely the thought that necessary truth could have *no* such bearing that led us to wonder how our beliefs about them could have been reliably arrived at; and that in turn led us to consider the Darwinian account as a way out of the difficulty. So the Darwinian solution will not work for truths to the effect that something *must* be the case.

But suppose we consider, not the belief that, if anything is sweet and poisonous, it *must* be poisonous, but the belief simply that, if anything is sweet and poisonous, it *is* poisonous. Then there is a second consideration which applies to such beliefs as well. Beliefs of this sort are highly general: they have implications about what will be true in the future as well as the past; what is true in other parts of the universe as well as here; what *would* have been true in circumstances which will never arise. In so far as these beliefs have been tested, they have, *of course*, only been tested in times up to the present, in limited places, in circumstances that have actually arisen. *Perhaps* (but only perhaps), if their implications on these occasions of testing had been wrong for the most part, we would not have survived. But that does not mean that they are correct. It remains possible, for all our survival shows, that some of their implications that have *not* been tested are false—even that most of them are. The falsity of *these* implications could have had no bearing on our survival. In short, evolutionary considerations provide no more reasons for supposing that our beliefs in necessary truths are well adapted to all possible circumstances, than for supposing that our lungs are well adapted to all possible circumstances.

I conclude that the Darwinian solution will not work for logical truths.

## Pre-established Harmony

This solution takes a very different turn. The general idea is that God arranges things in such a way that our methods of forming beliefs about necessary truths are reliable. He brings it about that there is (or is likely to be) a match between our beliefs and the facts, not because he arranges things so that the facts affect our beliefs, but, rather, because he gives us a disposition to have beliefs which are, as a matter of fact, true.[4] It would be a *little* bit like someone making a calculator. He designs it so that it gives the right answers, though it has no insight into the facts, nor is it in any other way directly affected by them.

There seem, though, to be two possibilities, depending on whether the facts are thought of as dependent on God's will or not. Either way we shall not be out of the woods.

Let us suppose that the facts in question are *not* dependent on God's will. Then how does God succeed in making our beliefs match the facts? Presumably because *he* knows the facts. But in that case the original problem about knowledge of such facts arises in the case of God. So have we made any progress? We might think that we had. We might think that the problem arises in our case because for *us* the knowledge in question is constituted by having beliefs. And so there is a problem about the reliability of our beliefs. But for God it is different, one might claim. His knowledge does not involve beliefs. It is simply an immediate apprehension of facts. But, even if this is so, the original problem remains. On this account it will still be the case that the facts affect *our* beliefs. It is just that they will not affect them directly. The position will be that the facts will affect our beliefs by way of God's apprehension of the facts. So, it is not that I want to say that this solution must be *wrong*. It is just that it will not be a solution which avoids the idea which seemed so difficult: the idea that necessary facts could affect what we contingently believe.

---

[4] This is the line taken by Leibniz and effectively by Descartes. See Ralph C. S. Walker, *Kant* (London: Routledge, 1978), ch. 12, and *The Coherence Theory of Truth*, chs. 4 and 11.

Let us suppose instead, then, that the facts are dependent on God's will. Perhaps, we might add, that is how *he* knows the facts. He knows them by knowing what he wills. But at any rate the story will be that he is able to provide for a connection between the facts and our ways of believing, by willing both. But there are still problems. In particular, on this view it would seem to follow that the supposed necessary facts will, after all, be *contingent*. It is true that one might, perhaps, argue that this need not be so; because it might be a matter of necessity that God wills what he does. But then we are back to the problem of how it is possible for God to know *this* necessary fact, that he wills such-and-such. Either God's knowledge involves belief, in which case we are back to the original problem; or it involves (say) just apprehension without belief. But that will not help either. It will still have to be that our beliefs are affected by the necessary fact about what God wills; indirectly, to be sure, by way of God's apprehension of the fact; but affected nonetheless. And, of course, it is no good saying that God does not *need* to know what he wills. If he does not know, we have no account of how his willing what he wills about the *facts* is connected with his willing what he wills about our *beliefs*.

### Grasping the Nettle

It looks as if there is nothing for it but to accept that necessary facts can affect contingent beliefs.[5] The alternative would be to come to the conclusion that we not only have no knowledge of necessary truths, we do not even have a good reason to believe that there are any truths—even *logical* truths. But it seems altogether harder to accept *that*.

Can we say any more? Well, though it is true that *one* account which would fit with accepting that necessary facts can affect contingent beliefs is the account that appeals to pre-established harmony, it is not the only possible account. Another possibility is that *we* have

---

[5] See Laurence BonJour, *In Defence of Pure Reason* (Cambridge: Cambridge University Press, 1998), 6.2.

some sort of more or less direct apprehension of the facts (or at any rate some of them). Could we say any more about it? Well, we could compare it with ordinary perception. Just as ordinary perception provides for the possibility of the shaping of our beliefs by contingent facts, so this sort of a priori perception provides for the possibility of the shaping of our beliefs by necessary facts. Beyond that there are various choices. Some philosophers think that ordinary perception is essentially just a causal process; some think that it involves an awareness of things which does not itself consist in a causal process, though it provides for a causal relation between our beliefs and the facts. There are the same sorts of choices in the case of a priori perception. Perhaps it is just a causal process; or perhaps it is not itself a causal process, but provides for a causal relation between our beliefs and the necessary facts. But we do not need to make a choice for the purposes of this chapter. It is enough to conclude that necessary facts *can* make a difference to what happens; they can make a difference to what we believe.

# 4

# Existence and Goodness

I HAVE ARGUED THAT ordinary thinking is committed to the existence of objective value; I have also argued that it is committed to the view that objective value is capable of making a difference to what happens, because it is capable of shaping our thinking. I have also noted that ordinary thinking believes in the existence of order. Is a belief in these three things, objective value, objective value that makes a difference, and order, enough to constitute religious belief? Well, there is at any rate is *something* that is missing; that is, a connection between objective value and order in general. Ordinary thinking is committed to a connection between value and thought, but not between value and the world as a whole. But now we can notice that there is, nonetheless, a *momentum* in the ordinary way of thought that can take us further than we have gone so far. We have accepted (in so far as we accept the commitments of ordinary thinking) that objective value makes a difference at the level of thought; and this opens at least the *possibility* that it may do so more generally. Metaphysically speaking this is, surely, not a very much bigger step. But is there anything that might lead us to take the step? The answer is that there is. It is something we have already identified as a crucial ingredient in scientific thinking; it is, in fact, what drives scientific thinking. It is the belief in intelligibility, the belief in explanation. We believe in things we cannot observe. We believe in laws of nature. We believe in these things, as I have said, because they provide an explanation of the evidence in question; because they render things intelligible. Well, then, this belief in intelligibility and explanation drives us to a belief in a universe which obeys such-and-such laws. It may also drive us to ask, 'Why is there a universe such as this? Why are the laws of nature as they are?' But although what drives scientific thinking may lead to these questions, ordinary scientific answers are, of course, not available. Ordinary scientific thinking may come up with the laws; it may even tell us that the universe had such-and-such a beginning, or had no beginning. But it will not answer our further questions, '*Why* is all this so?', 'Why are the laws of nature as they are?', 'Why is there anything that obeys these laws?' And perhaps it is worth emphasizing that the possibility of asking these questions does not depend on whether one thinks that the universe has a beginning or not; whether, let us say, one subscribes to a big bang theory, or a steady state theory. Fairly evidently, such beliefs have no bearing on the question of why the laws are as they are. But, equally, they have no bearing on why there is a universe. Even if one believes that there has *always* been a universe, one can still ask, 'Why?' Now, of course, one does not *need* to ask these further questions, 'Why?' One need not; but the natural momentum of the search for explanation may lead one to. Again, one may ask the questions, but think that there is no answer; one may think that all that can be said is that things just are so. But, equally, one may notice that there is a possible answer, an answer which is already metaphysically available. We have seen that the belief in objective value commits us to the belief that this objective value can make a difference. We have seen that this opens up the possibility that it might make a difference not only at the level of thought, but more generally. Well, then, we could take advantage of this possibility. Impelled by the natural momentum of the search for explanation, we could take a further step. We could say that there is a universe such as this, obeying laws such as these, *because it is good that it should be so*.[1]

---

[1] This is John Leslie's view in his *Value and Existence*. However, the line I take differs from Leslie's in two respects. The first is that Leslie regards the explanation of the existence of the world in terms of value as being a unique explanation, and not, therefore, to be argued for by appeal to the existence of similar explanations in other fields. But I do not think it is unique. It is an explanation of the same general sort as applies to the explanation of many beliefs we all have about good and bad. The second way in which I differ from Leslie will emerge in the next chapter. I believe that the explanation of the existence of the universe directly in terms of its goodness, though it is to be distinguished from an explanation in terms of a personal God, amounts nonetheless to an explanation in terms of God's will. I should also mention that A. C. Ewing has argued that the existence of *God* should be explained in terms of the fact that it is

The step is not compulsory, but it is possible:

A man that looks on glasse
On it may stay his eye,
Or if he pleaseth, through it passe,
And then the heav'n espie.[2]

And, I suggest, it is not only possible, but natural.

It is natural not just to believe in order and in objective value, but also to believe that this value explains not only some particular things that go on in the world, but the order itself and the world itself. It is a natural belief, and it is clearly, broadly speaking, a *religious* belief. But does it yet amount to a belief in God? That is a question which I shall defer till the next chapter. For the rest of this chapter I want to consider a little further what is to be said for (and against) the idea that the existence of a universe such as this is to be explained by appeal to goodness: by appeal to the fact that it is good that there should be such a universe.

## God as Mediator

The belief that I have called natural, the belief that I am defending, is a belief that the existence of the universe is to be explained by appeal to its goodness. But it is, of course, not the only sort of account that appeals to the goodness of the universe. Such an appeal is made by any account which explains the existence of the universe in terms of its creation by a good God. But commonly an account of this sort thinks of the explanation in terms of goodness as *mediated* by God. On such an account, the universe exists because God created it, and he created it because it was good that there should be such a universe. Should we prefer an account which introduces a mediating

good that he should exist. See his 'Two "Proofs" of God's Existence', *Religious Studies* 1 (1966), 29–46.

[2] George Herbert, *The Elixir*, from *The Works of George Herbert*, ed. F. E. Hutchinson (Oxford: Clarendon Press, 1941), 184.

God into the explanation to an account which does not? I shall argue that we should not.

Why might one prefer an account which introduces a mediating God? Well, the most obvious reason would be that one took the view that the *only* way in which objective value could make a difference was at the level of thought. For then, if one wished to explain the existence of the world by appeal to goodness, one would be obliged to suppose that the explanation involved an appeal to a mind which apprehended the goodness; so one would naturally be led to the idea of a mediating God. But, if one is really committed to the idea of objective value, of value which is not constituted by facts about minds, it is quite unobvious why one should take such a view. Given the commitment, which I have urged that we have, to the possibility that objective value can make a difference to the way we think, it is not at all clear why it should not be in principle possible for it to affect the way things are more generally.

But one might prefer the account which introduces a mediating God for a slightly different reason. One might accept that it might be possible *in principle* for objective value to make a difference other than at the level of thought; one might, however, be impressed by the fact that we have no experience of its making a difference in any other way; and one might therefore prefer an account according to which objective value operated in a familiar way, rather than in a way which was quite novel. But I do not think that this is a good reason. In the first place, it is not at all clear that what is proposed by the account which introduces a mediating God is, taken as a whole, closer to our experience than the account according to which the goodness of the universe has its effect directly. It may well be that we do not have any experience of goodness affecting things other than minds; but we also have no experience of minds creating laws of nature; or, indeed of minds creating anything, except possibly thoughts, *ex nihilo*. So, even if the notion of a mind's perceiving that something is good is a relatively familiar one, the notion of a mind's creating a universe is a very unfamiliar one, and (or so it seems to me) at least as unfamiliar as the notion that the goodness of the universe is directly responsible for its existence; so, at any rate, it is not to be preferred simply on the grounds of familiarity. In the second place, the account which introduces a mediating God leaves more unexplained than the account which does not: namely the existence of the mediating God.

Of course, if we had *other* reasons for supposing that there was a God who was capable of creating the universe, this need not be an objection. Now, I do not wish to deny that there may be other reasons for believing in such a God. But my concern in this chapter, and indeed in this book, is to see what we may reasonably believe without appealing to such other reasons; and, in particular, to consider what sort of God we may reasonably believe in without appealing to such other reasons. That is to say, for my present purposes, I am supposing that that our reason for believing in a mediating God would be simply that we think that the existence of the universe is to be explained in terms of its goodness. So, given that the account which involves the hypothesis of a mediating God does not do a better job of explaining the existence of the universe than the account which does not, we should apply Ockham's razor. We should prefer the latter account.

### Explanation and Laws

I have argued that the account which does not involve a mediating God is to be preferred to the account which does. But we ought to notice that there are two difficulties for both accounts. The first difficulty is that both accounts seek to explain the existence of the world by appeal to its goodness. But the problem is that the world is not in all respects good; there are bad things about it too. I shall address this difficulty in Chapter 6. The second difficulty lies in an account of causation, particularly associated with David Hume, which connects the existence of a causal relation between two things with the existence of a law relating them.[3] The account claims that if one event, A, is the cause of another event, B, it must be that there is a *law* which

---

[3] See Hume, *A Treatise of Human Nature*, Bk. I, pt. III, sect. XIV, and *An Enquiry Concerning Human Understanding*, sect. VII.

implies that, whenever an event sufficiently like A occurs, in circumstances sufficiently similar, there will always be an event like B.

I will say something shortly about the nature of the difficulty which this account of causation presents. But first we should notice that it might be thought that it could not threaten my preferred account at all; because on that account there is no attempt to explain one *event* in terms of another. Rather, the fact that it would be good that there should be a world such as this is presented as explaining the fact that there is such a world. And certainly the fact that it would be good that there should be such a world is not itself a matter of the occurrence of an *event*; and, what is more, the thing that we are hoping to explain need not involve any event—one might think of the world and the laws of nature as always having existed. And, even on the account which involves a mediating God, one might perhaps think of his creative act as not being something that took place in time, and therefore as not, strictly speaking, involving any event. And, perhaps for that reason, one might think that the explanation being offered was not a *causal* explanation. So, could we simply ignore the question of whether the causation of one event by another of necessity involved the existence of a law? Now, actually I do not think that it is at all obvious that causation is always of one event by another; nor that the explanation which we are considering is not a causal explanation. But, even if I am wrong about this, it would be a mistake if we did not first look at the *reasons* for thinking that causation between events involved the existence of laws. Because otherwise we could not be assured that there was not a good reason to suppose that the sort of explanation which we are hoping to provide does not also involve the existence of laws, even if it is not a causal explanation.[4]

But why should we worry if our explanation involves the existence of laws? The reason is this. We are hoping to explain the existence of laws of nature in terms of the fact that it would be good that there

---

[4] Richard Swinburne argues that the explanation of the result of a person's basic action in terms of his intention is not to be analysed in terms of a law relating that intention to that result. See his *The Existence of God* (Oxford: Clarendon Press, 1979), 36–42.

should be such laws—with or without the involvement of a mediating God. If that explanation itself were to involve the existence of a law connecting facts about goodness with facts about the laws of nature, there would seem to be two problems. The first problem is this. Such a law would not, of course, be one of the laws of nature whose existence it would supposedly be explaining. Nor would it be a necessary truth—at least on my preferred account—for, if it were, it would seem to make the existence of a world like this a necessary truth. So it would be a contingent truth. But that would mean that its existence would constitute an unexplained fact which might be no easier to accept than unexplained laws of nature. The second, and perhaps the more important, problem would be that it would be difficult to see what such a law could be, given that it would have to explain the existence of the world with all its apparently contingent features. It might be different if we thought that the actual world was the best possible world; for then we might suppose that the law said that the best possible world would exist. But it is, to say the least, rather difficult to suppose that this *is* the best possible world. Alternatively, one might suppose that the law was that *any* good world would exist.[5] But to accept that would mean accepting that there actually exists (or has existed) an infinity of different worlds. Perhaps that is possible; perhaps it is actually so. But one might feel happier with the proffered explanation if it did not involve any such commitment.

It is not as if these difficulties are simply the consequence of my preferred account, and that they would disappear on the account that introduced a mediating God. It is true that the origin of some of the apparently contingent features of the world could be located in the nature of the creator—perhaps the universal law would be that any being with just *this* nature would produce a world like this. But the more we located the contingency in the nature of the creator, the less satisfying would it seem to accept as an unexplained fact the *existence* of a creator just like this. Perhaps we could see how it might be the case that a creator like this would create a world like this; but why should there *be* a creator like this? So it would be as well to consider

---

[5] Or perhaps, as one of the anonymous readers for Oxford University Press has suggested, the law might be that the best sum of worlds exists.

the question of whether the considerations that lead people to say
that causation between events involve laws are cogent; and, if so,
whether they apply equally well to the sort of explanation I am offering.

We should notice first that it is necessary to advance arguments
that causation between events always involves laws. I mean that a
superficial consideration of what we mean by 'cause' does not reveal
any such involvement; compare this with the case of what we mean
by 'bachelor', where a superficial examination reveals that, of *course*,
one cannot be a bachelor without being unmarried. As far as a superficial consideration goes, there seems to be no contradiction in supposing that an event of type A should cause an event of type B on
one occasion, but fail to cause it on another (or, indeed, on *any*
other), even though the circumstances were the same. One might
think that this would never happen, but it does not immediately strike
one as involving the sort of impossibility that would be involved in
the supposition that on some occasions 2 + 2 = 5. So let us consider
whether there are arguments to show that, in spite of appearances, it
is actually impossible that something should cause something on one
occasion, but fail to do so on another in identical circumstances.

The most important argument is this. There is certainly *more* to A's
causing B than A's happening and B's happening. What could this
'more' be? One possibility is precisely that the 'more' consists in there
being a law relating things like A, in circumstances like this, to things
like B. One might wonder, of course, why *anything* needs to be said.
Why not suppose that causation is a relation between events that is
not to be analysed any further? The general answer, I think, is just
that philosophers do not much like accepting the existence of
unanalysable things if they can be avoided. There is also, in some
cases (and this was true of Hume), a view about the origin of concepts which seems to tell against the possibility that our concept of
causation is unanalysable. The view is that all concepts are either
given in experience or are constructed by simple logical operations
from concepts given in experience.[6] To which is added the claim that

---

[6] Hume, *A Treatise of Human Nature*, Bk. I, pt. I, sect. I, and *An Enquiry Concerning Human Understanding*, sect. II.

the concept of causation is *not* given in experience. However, I shall not discuss this latter motivation beyond reiterating that *nothing* is given in experience. So, does the extra that differentiates A's causing B from their both simply occurring consist in the fact that they are related by laws in the way I have mentioned? The answer is that it cannot at any rate consist *simply* in this. The reason is that causation is an asymmetric relation: that is to say, if A caused B, then B cannot have caused A.[7] But to be related by a law is a symmetrical relation—if A is related to B by a law, then B is related to A by the same law. Of course, some laws may themselves be asymmetrical. Newton's laws are not; but, for all that, had Newton been right, this would not have meant that the movement of this billiard ball was not the cause of the movement of that one. So laws, by themselves, cannot account for the asymmetry in causation. What does, then? Well, an obvious answer is that what accounts for the asymmetry is the fact that the effect always follows the cause. So, what makes A the cause of B is that they are related by laws in the appropriate way and, in addition, A happened before B. But this cannot be right. It may indeed be true that it is impossible for a cause to be later than its effect (though, as it happens, I do not think it is); but, if so, it is not just a *trivial* fact, obvious to someone who simply thinks about what the word 'cause' means; the fact, if it is a fact, that a cause cannot follow its effect is not like the fact that a bachelor cannot be married.[8] Sometimes people pray about the past—'Please God, let it not be that John was on the *Titanic.*' One may perhaps think that it is irrational for them to think that they can make any difference to what happened by their prayers; but it would certainly not be like my praying that I should become a bachelor while remaining married. So, even if the effect does always follow the cause, what *makes* A the cause of B cannot be just this, together with the fact that they are related by laws in the appropriate way. It might be worth adding that on some views the impossibility that the cause should precede the effect is to be explained by the fact that the temporal order is dictated by the causal

    [7] See J. L. Mackie, *The Cement of the Universe: A Study of Causation* (Oxford: Clarendon Press, 1974), ch. 7.
    [8] Mackie, *The Cement of the Universe*, 161–2.

order, rather than vice versa: so that what makes A the cause of B, rather than B the cause of A, cannot be that A is earlier than B.[9]

So, what differentiates A's being the cause of B from their both simply occurring cannot be simply that they are related by laws. But, if the supposition that they must be related by laws does not, after all, provide the solution, the argument that they must be related by laws collapses. For the argument was based on the claim that the supposition *would* provide the solution.

There is another argument which can be dealt with rather more quickly. The argument is that, if someone claimed that A caused B on a certain occasion, and that no other factors were relevant, we would think that we had disproved his claim if we reproduced A, and B did not occur. But in fact that does not show that we are treating causation as *necessarily* involving laws. It need only be that we believe that, *as a matter of fact*, laws determine what causes what.

There is third argument which has to do with the nature of explanation. It goes like this. If A caused B, the occurrence of A explains why B happens. But, for the occurrence of A to explain the occurrence of B, it must be the case that B was bound to happen in those circumstances, given A. That is to say, there must be a law according to which B was bound to happen. This idea is closely related to the idea that, if there is an explanation of an occurrence in terms of what went before, it would have been possible in principle to have predicted it. Clearly this claim about explanation could be extended to take in the case we are particularly interested in, even if that explanation is not a causal explanation. It could be claimed that whenever one thing is explained in terms of another, there must be a law according to which the thing explained was bound to be the case, given that the thing doing the explaining was the case (together, perhaps, with other relevant facts).

Is this claim about explanation correct? It does not seem so. Here is one example. Consider Schrödinger's cat. A cat is put in a box with a barrel of explosive, which will be set off if a certain subatomic event occurs. Now, whether the event will or will not occur is not

---

[9] See, for instance, Richard Swinburne, *The Christian God* (Oxford: Clarendon Press, 1994), 81–90.

determined by any law. There is a *probability* that it will occur, but
there is also a probability that it will not. Suppose that it does occur,
and the unfortunate cat is killed. We shall surely think that the cat was
killed because it was put in the box. That is to say, we shall treat the
fact that it was put in the box as providing an *explanation* of its death.
But no law determined that it would die. Of course, it is true that
there is in a sense not a *complete* explanation. There is no explanation for the fact that, as a matter of fact, the undetermined event
occurred as opposed to not occurring. But that does not mean that
there is *no* explanation for the death. And, for what it is worth, one
need not even suppose that the barrel *could not* have exploded unless
it had been triggered by the undetermined event. One might suppose
that it *could* have exploded anyway (the quantum world being what it
is). That supposition does not mean we have no explanation. It is true
that there *is* a law in this case—a probabilistic law. So it might be suggested that a law is indeed needed if there is to be an explanation; it
is just that it need not be a deterministic law. But we should note that
the mere existence of such a law does not as such give us an explanation. For suppose that two events, A and B, occurred; and suppose
that, in virtue of a probabilistic law, the occurrence of event B was
more likely given the occurrence of event A than it would have been
in its absence. That in itself does not mean that B occurred *because*
A did (even in the absence of any other relevant factors); nor in itself
does it mean that the occurrence of B was to be explained by reference to the occurrence of A. But in that case we may well conclude
that, given that the existence of a law is not enough to provide us with
an explanation, we have no good reason to suppose that it is even necessary.

Here is another example. We can often explain people's actions in
terms of their beliefs. So, for instance, we can explain my moving my
arm by reference to the fact that I thought it would be useful to move
it. But surely we need not suppose that my moving my arm was *bound*
to occur, given that thought in those circumstances; we need not suppose that it was *necessitated*. That would be tantamount to supposing that my decision was determined by prior factors. And, although
some people do think that human actions are all determined, it does
not seem that the very fact that we think that an action can be

explained by reference to an agent's beliefs commits us to such a view. We may be wrong; perhaps we are committed to such a view. But, if so, some further argument needs to be presented to show that we are wrong. So, here we have another counterexample to the claim about explanation. Now, it is true that one might object to this as a relevant counterexample for the following reason. One might concede that we can explain my actions by reference to my beliefs without supposing that any laws are involved which are such that, given those beliefs and the circumstances, I was bound to act as I did. But, one might claim, this is because a particular account of the nature of the explanation is available here, which is not available in (ordinary) cases of causation, nor available in the case envisaged by my favoured account. The explanation, it may be said, goes like this. My belief that it would be useful to raise my arm explains my action simply because it explains why, given my beliefs, my action would be rational (or would fulfil my desires, perhaps). However, that account cannot be right. The mere fact that, given my belief that it would be useful to raise my arm, it would be rational to raise it, does not explain why I actually *did* raise it. For it to explain that, it needs to be the case that I raised it *because* I thought it would be useful; it needs to be the case that my belief led to my action.

I conclude that we have no overwhelming reason to give up the idea that it is possible for A to cause B without there being a law connecting them. And no overwhelming reason to suppose that, if the fact that it would be good for there to be a world such as this is to explain the world's existence, there must be a law connecting the two.

## How Good an Explanation?

I am defending an account which explains the existence of the world by reference to its goodness. I have suggested that this account is a natural account. But is it, after all, to be preferred to an account which says that there is *no* explanation for the fact that there is a world such as this?

Now, first we should notice no account can go on for ever. At some

stage any explanation is going to have to content itself with asserting
that something is so, without going on to provide an explanation of
*this* fact. One important factor, then, in how satisfying we may find
explanations will be how satisfying we find these stopping points. It
is true that there is one sort of stopping point that is particularly well
suited to being satisfying: that is, a stopping point which appeals to
a necessary truth. If, in answer to our questioning, '*Why* is this so?',
we come up against the fact that it could not have been otherwise, we
are liable to be satisfied. This is particularly the case if we can *see* that
it must be so. So it would be rather nice if *all* explanations could have,
as their stopping points, nothing but necessary truths. Alas, however
nice this might be, such an explanation is not to be found for *contingent* facts, for things that could have been otherwise. The reason is
just that, if anything is the logical consequence of necessary truths,
it must itself be a necessary truth. So, in any explanation of a contingent fact, there is bound to be some contingency. So, since it is
surely a contingent fact that there is a universe such as this, it follows
that any explanation of this fact is going involve some stopping
points which are themselves contingent. And this is going to mean
that we should not always expect to find agreement on whether one
explanation is better than another. Different people may find different stopping points satisfactory. It is for this reason that I earlier
represented as not compulsory the move which appealed to the
explanation of the existence of the world in terms of the fact that it
was good that there should be such a world. Some people may find it
perfectly satisfying instead to accept as a stopping point the existence
of a world such as this. Or at least they may find it as satisfying as any
alternative they have considered. In particular, they may regard it as
more satisfying than the explanation that is offered in terms of objective value. And although one *might* claim that one of these explanations just *is* better than another, so that one *ought* to accept one rather
than another, and so that it is *rational* to accept one rather than
another, one might equally regard this as a pointless, even misleading, claim. Because it might suggest that there are generally accepted
standards of rationality according to which one view is rational and
the other is not. And this is surely not the case.

Nonetheless, there *is*, I think, some reason to prefer the account I am defending to the account which accepts the existence of the world as a unexplained fact. The reason is that this account serves to unify what would otherwise be two unrelated facts. On the one hand, we have human thoughts and actions which are to be explained in part by reference to what is good; not just what we *believe* to be good—facts about goodness must play a role, as I argued in the previous chapter. On the other hand we have the workings of nature, where, except to the extent that humans intervene, facts about goodness play no part. On the account I am proposing, these two otherwise unrelated areas are unified by the role of the good. And unification is a mark of a good explanation.

To this it is worth adding that there is a difficult problem which could be solved by appeal to goodness, and in particular by the account I propose.[10] This has to do with the rationality of our scientific procedures. In the previous chapter, I argued that we need to suppose that there is some connection between necessary facts and our ways of arriving at them if we are to be rational in placing in them such confidence as we do. There is a similar requirement in the case of the beliefs we form on the basis of evidence. I am not thinking now of our belief that such-and-such evidence supports such-and-such a conclusion. That, as I have said, is a belief about a necessary fact. I am thinking rather of the beliefs we form on the basis of evidence which we take to support our conclusion; beliefs, in particular, about the laws of nature. It seems that, if we are to be rational in placing confidence, *some* degree of confidence, in our ways of arriving at these beliefs, there must be some connection between the laws of nature themselves and our practices. As I said in the first chapter, the concepts that we bring to bear upon the world are our concepts; there is no *necessity* that these concepts classify things in the world in a way which has any bearing on the way in which the world actually operates. So, how could there be a connection between our ways of thinking and the way the world is?

The obvious solution to consider would be a Darwinian one. It is, one might suggest, natural selection which has made it likely that our ways of classifying bear sufficient relation to the way the world is,

---

[10]  I am indebted here to Ralph C. S. Walker. See his *Kant*, ch. 12.

because, if they had not been on approximately the right lines, we would not have survived. But this explanation will not work here, any more than it worked in connection with necessary facts. The problem is that our ways of classifying the world, and the sorts of beliefs we have formed about the world on that basis, have *of course* survived testing only in *actual* circumstances, up to the *present*. So the fact that we have not come to grief so far does not mean that we are on the right lines. We may be badly wrong. There is indeed an infinite number of completely incorrect ways in which we might have classified things, which are compatible with our surviving so far.[11] Now, at this stage one might protest that, to be sure, we *may* have been classifying things incorrectly; but that does not mean that the fact that we have survived so far does not make it *probable* that we will continue to survive; and, so, probable that we have been on the right lines. It is a familiar fact about scientific reasoning on the basis of evidence that the evidence is always compatible with the falsity of conclusions we base on it. That familiar fact does not prevent its being at least probable that the conclusion is correct (or somewhere near correct).

But, unfortunately, this reply will not defuse the problem. As I pointed out in Chapter 1, in so far as we are rational, we take ourselves to be entitled to draw conclusions on the basis of evidence just to the extent that we think that the conclusion helps to explain the evidence, or is implied by an explanation which helps to explain the evidence. So, do our past successes provide good evidence that we are thinking on the right lines? The answer is, only to the extent that they provide evidence for something that would *explain* the fact that we have been thinking on the right lines. But that is just the problem. We do not *have* any explanation of how our thinking could have been brought into line with the world. But, one might protest again, is it *really* true that an appeal to natural selection will not serve? Maybe natural selection does not guarantee that our thinking is not badly amiss; but does it not make it *improbable* that it is badly amiss? Because surely it is probable that a way of thinking that is amiss will not survive. The answer to this is that, although it may be improbable

---

[11] This is one implication of Nelson Goodman's tale of 'grue' and 'bleen'. See his *Fact, Fiction and Forecast*, ch. 3.

that a way of thinking which is amiss will survive *in the long run*, that does not mean that it is improbable that it should have survived until now.

Nonetheless, we *do* think that our ways of thinking are reliable. So how does the connection between them and the world arise? One solution which was available in the case of necessary truth is surely not available here. We do not have an a priori apprehension of the laws of nature. But another solution *is* available, the solution in terms of pre-established harmony. Put in terms of the account which introduces a mediating God, the explanation could be that God was responsible both for the laws of nature and for our ways of thinking. Perhaps *he* is responsible for the connection. Put in terms of the account I am offering, perhaps it is like this: not only are the laws of nature as they are because it is good that they should be so, but our ways of thinking bear some relation to the way the world is because it is good that there should be such a relation. Why is it good? Because it is good that we should be equipped to survive in the long run? Perhaps this is part of the answer; but it is surely not the whole answer. We could have been well equipped without any scientific views. The chief reason is, surely, that it is good to *understand*. And we would not have any way of achieving an understanding of the world if our ways of thinking were badly amiss.

I conclude that it is, at the very least, rational to believe that there exists a universe such as this because it is good that such a universe should exist; at any rate, it is rational if the presence of bad things in the universe does not render it irrational.

# 5

# Goodness and God

IN THE PREVIOUS CHAPTER I defended an explanation of the existence of the world which appealed to the fact that it is good that there should be such a world. In particular I argued that the explanation which appealed directly to goodness was to be preferred to an explanation which introduced a mediating God. Does this imply that we should prefer an account in which God plays no part? I do not believe so. Preference for an account which does not involve God conceived in a certain way does not require the acceptance of an account which does not involve God at all. I shall argue that, on the contrary, our account of the existence of the world provides us with the foundation for a satisfying conception of God. To help us to see how this might be so I shall start by saying something about the relation between God and morality.

## God and Morality

God is commonly thought of not only as creator of the world but also as its ruler. In particular it is commonly thought that it is God who determines what is right or wrong, good or bad. God is sovereign. And one of the problems with the idea of a mediating God is precisely that it represents God as acting in the light of his apprehension of what is *independently* good. He is not, on this view, entirely sovereign; he is constrained in what he does by something which is not determined by him. Now, one might think that this problem was fairly easily solved. One might think that it could be solved by pointing out that God is, of course, subject to the laws of logic.

He cannot do what is logically impossible—of course not: if God could do something, it would be something that could be done; so it would not be impossible. But this does not derogate from his sovereignty. So why should it be supposed that being subject to laws (so to speak) of right and wrong should derogate from his sovereignty? It might even be suggested that the basic laws of morality *are* just logical truths.[1] But this would as it stands be a poor answer. There is indeed an anodyne sense in which God is subject to the laws of logic—namely, that he cannot do what cannot be done. But the problem about the laws of morality is that he would seem to be subject to them in a different sense: it is not that he *cannot* do anything other than what is morally right, it is that he *should not* do anything other than what is morally right. And, indeed, there is a parallel, and not obviously anodyne, sense in which he might be said to be subject to the laws of logic: namely, that he *should* not think illogically. However, a rather different comparison could be made between God's relation to right and wrong and his relation to logic. It might be said that, *of course*, God could not determine the laws of logic, for the laws of logic are necessary truths; they could not have been other than they are; but in the same way, God *could not* determine the basic facts about right and wrong, because they also are necessary truths. Now the trouble with *this* answer (assuming that it is right) is, one might think, that it does not so much solve the problem as concede that it is insoluble. It amounts to saying that we have no choice but to concede that God's role would be bound to be secondary in importance to the facts about good and bad. His role is *bound* to be that of mediator only; he *could not* be sovereign. It amounts to saying that one of the key features in many people's conception of God is incoherent.

It is true that, even if one were to accept that the basic facts about good and bad were not determined by God, one need not think that nothing to do with morality was determined by him. A certain division of labour might be possible. One might, for instance, distinguish

---

[1] For this view see Richard Swinburne, *The Coherence of Theism* (Oxford: Clarendon Press, 1977), ch. 11. His argument for this position, however, in itself supports only the view that they are necessary truths.

between what it is our moral *duty* to do (and, perhaps, what it is right
to do, and wrong not to do) and what it is *good* to do.[2] And one might
claim that, while God does not determine what it is good to do, he
does determine what it is our duty to do. Our duty is determined by
what God commands us to do. I shall return to this later when I discuss the idea that God commands us.

But is it possible that God might in fact determine the basic facts
about good and bad?

There is one suggestion about how this might be so which I shall
mention in passing. The suggestion is that God determines what is
good in the same way as the standard metre stick in Paris determines
what is a metre long. Just as being a metre long is constituted by being
the same length as the standard metre stick, so being good is constituted by being (appropriately) like God.[3] But I do not think that this
comparison with the standard metre stick can possibly be right—at
least as far as my own usage of the word 'good' is concerned. The reason is that it is pretty obvious to me, and I assume to most reflective
users of the word 'metre', that being a metre in length is constituted
by being suitably related to the length of *some* standard object (or
objects): by being the same length as the object or by being some mul-
tiple of the length, presumably. *Which* the standard object or objects
are, one may not know; but it is evident that there must be some if the
notion of a metre is well defined. Now the crucial point is that it is
the *meaning* of the word 'metre' which determines that there must be
some standard in the case of metres; so if the relation between goodness and God were parallel to that between being a metre long and
the standard metre, it would be part of the meaning of the word
'good' that a standard was involved. But no such thing is part of the
meaning I attach to the word 'good'; nor, I believe, is it part of the
meaning that most people attach to the word.

There is another type of suggestion, however, which is more obviously related to the idea of sovereignty. One version associates good-

[2] See William P. Alston, 'Some Suggestions for Divine Command Theorists', in his
*Divine Nature and Human Language* (Ithaca, N.Y.: Cornell University Press, 1989);
first published in Michael Beaty (ed.), *Christian Theism and the Problems of Philosophy*
(Notre Dame, Ind.: University of Notre Dame Press, 1989).
[3] See Alston, 'Some Suggestions for Divine Command Theorists'.

ness and badness with God's commands: those things are good which God commands us to do; those things are bad which God commands us not to do. Such a view is often referred to as 'the divine command theory'. Another version associates goodness and badness with God's will: those things are good which God wills should be; those things are bad which God wills should not be. Let us call this 'the divine will theory'. I shall concentrate on the latter version; but both versions share a fundamental problem.

First, we should be clear about what the divine will theory is actually claiming. It is making a claim about the basic facts about value. But we can distinguish two rather different sorts of claims. The first is a substantive claim about what the facts actually are. It might go like this. We are inclined to think that there are a number of basic facts about value—for instance (say), that one ought to keep promises, and that there is something wrong about causing unnecessary pain. But we are wrong. There is only one basic fact, namely that it is good that what God wills should come into being. The second makes a metaphysical claim about the nature of basic facts about value, whatever those facts might be. It might go like this. It is indeed a basic fact about value that there is something wrong about causing unnecessary pain (say); that is to say, the wrongness of doing this is not contingent on some other facts about the world. But this basic fact just *consists* in the fact that God wills that there should not be unnecessary suffering. On the first sort of claim, God is not responsible for the basic facts about value. When he wills, he does not bring such a fact into existence. He does indeed bring it about that there are certain things that are good, which would not have been otherwise; but they owe their goodness to two things: the basic fact about value that what God wills is good, and the fact that God willed these things. This might be compared with what happens when I make a promise—to pay you five pounds, let us say. I bring it about that there is something I ought to do (pay you five pounds), but I do not bring about any basic fact about what ought to be done; rather, that I ought to pay you is a consequence of two facts: what I promised, for which I am responsible, and the fact that one ought to do what one promises (say), for which I am not responsible. On the first sort of claim, then, God brings it about by willing that certain things are good in much the same way as I bring it about by promising that I should do certain things. It is the *second* sort of claim that I am interested in, the claim about the metaphysical status of basic facts about value.

Let me first mention two criticisms, which are sometimes levelled at the divine will theory, to which there are perfectly adequate answers. The first says that it is perfectly obvious that, whatever the differences may be between the atheist and the believer, they use the word 'good' in the same sense; and it is perfectly obvious also that this sense does not involve any reference to God. The quick answer to this objection is that the divine will theory need not say anything about the *meaning* of the word 'good'; in particular, it need not claim that there is any reference in the *meaning* of the word to God.[4] The second criticism says that, if this theory were right, we would have to have beliefs about God's will, if we were to have any basis for our beliefs about what was good; but actually, if anything, it is the other way round: we believe that he wills our happiness (say) because we believe that it is good that we should be happy. And anyway, the criticism continues, how does the atheist arrive at his beliefs? Or are they completely unfounded? But this criticism is again misguided. The divine will theory is a theory about the nature of the basic facts about value; it is not, as such, a theory about our beliefs in such facts. Perhaps, nonetheless, the theorist had better say something about our beliefs to explain how they might be *reliable* on his view. However, he could say that our beliefs about goodness are capable of being reliable because God has given us minds which tend to think of as good just those things that he wills. Not that we tend to think of them *as willed by God*; just that we tend to think of them as good. And this account could apply to the atheist as well as to the believer.

The divine will theory is, however, open to an objection which is not so easily answered. The objection is that, if the divine will theory is right, this must mean that it could have been perfectly all right to torture babies (say); indeed, it could have been a *good* thing to do. It might have been all right, even good, because God could have willed

<hr/>

[4] See, for instance, Robert M. Adams, 'Divine Command Metaethics Modified Again', in his *The Virtue of Faith* (Oxford: Oxford University Press, 1987); first published in *Journal of Religious Ethics*, 7 (1979), 66–79.

that babies should be tortured. And (the objection continues) it is no good replying that he would not have willed anything so evil, because on the divine will theory nothing is good or evil independently of what God wills. On the contrary, if he *had* willed such a thing, it would *not* have been evil. Has the divine will theory a reply?

There are, I think, two possible replies. The first reply concedes that it is a consequence of the theory that it could have been all right to torture babies, but denies that this is an unacceptable consequence. It *seems* unacceptable just because it seems so awful to us to torture babies. And indeed it *is* awful. But it is awful just because God wills that such a thing should not happen; and it seems awful because God has made it seem so to our minds. What we fail to notice is that God could have made it all right, and could have made it seem so to us. But I do not think that this reply will do. It is not just that it seems to us that it is awful to torture babies; it seems to us that *it could not have been otherwise*. And this is inconsistent with what the reply claims. What I am appealing to, of course, is the *necessity* of basic facts about value, which I argued for in Chapter 2. And the objection to the reply is that it represents a supposed basic fact about value as *contingent*—contingent on God's will. At this point, the person who offers this reply may call into doubt this claim about necessity. My belief that such facts are necessary is surely not infallible. Indeed it is not. But I shall need very powerful arguments to the contrary to make it rational to abandon this belief. It is not enough for the replier simply to point out the bare possibility of error.[5]

The first reply, then, is unsatisfactory. The second reply attempts to avoid its defects by claiming that the objection is wrong when it claims that, on the divine will theory, it could have been all right to torture babies on the grounds that God could have willed such a thing. This reply says that in fact God could *not* have willed such a thing, because to do so would have been inconsistent with his nature. But at first sight this reply also seems quite unsatisfactory. This is

---

[5] For a defence of the view that God is responsible for necessary truths, see Descartes's letter of 2 May 1644 to Mesland, *The Philosophical Writings of Descartes*, vol. iii, trans. J. Cottingham, R. Stoothoff, D. Murdoch, and A. Kenny (Cambridge: Cambridge University Press, 1991), 235 (AT IV 118–19).

because it seems hard to see how his nature could make such a thing impossible. For, it seems, we cannot say that the crucial feature of God's nature is that he wills what is *good*; if that were to provide an answer, surely things must be good *in advance of* God's willing them. Otherwise all we are being told is that he wills what he wills; which is no sort of answer. Nor does not seem likely that an answer can be found by trying to derive God's willing what he wills from *other* features of his nature—his omnipotence or omniscience, say.[6] One could, it is true, resort to saying that it is a fundamental fact that God of necessity wills those things that he wills—such as the happiness of his creatures, say. But this answer is far from unproblematic; for we certainly have no intuitions about necessity to help us see how it might be so. As long, that is, as we resist the illicit thought that these things are *good*, and that is why he wills them. But there is a further difficulty. Even if we were to concede the necessity of God's willing what he wills, it would *still* be the case that on this account there might have been nothing wrong with torturing babies, or so it seems. For, what if God had not existed? In that case, on this account, there would have been no basic facts about value at all—nothing right, nothing wrong, nothing good, nothing bad.[7] Of course this problem could in its turn be dissolved if one could claim that God exists of necessity; in particular, if one could claim that it could not have failed to be true that there was a being who willed these things. But, again, our intuitions about necessity do not help us to see that this is so. It does not *seem* to be a necessary truth. It *seems*, if true, contingently true.

There is, however, an answer. Now the divine will theory may be

[6] Richard Swinburne does indeed think that it follows from the fact that God is omniscient and perfectly free that he can do no wrong, and hence that he cannot command wrongdoing. See his *The Coherence of Theism*, 204. But it is crucial to his argument for this that the basic moral truths are necessary truths, and not a consequence of God's will.

[7] In fact, it is part of Adams's view that, if there is not a *loving* God, then nothing is ethically wrong, or obligatory, or permitted. See his 'Divine Command Metaethics Modified Again', 129; also his 'A Modified Divine Command Theory of Ethical Wrongness', in his *The Virtue of Faith* (Oxford: Oxford University Press, 1987), first published in Gene Outka and John P. Reeder (eds.), *Religion and Morality* (Garden City, N.Y.: Anchor, 1973). If I am right, this is an objection to his view.

thought of as identifying the basic fact that something is good with the fact that God wills it. That is to say, it may be thought of as saying that its being the case that something is good, where it is a basic fact that this is so, is one and the same thing as God's willing whatever it is. For example, let us suppose that it is a basic fact that it is good that we should be happy; then the divine will theory says that its being good that we should be happy is one and the same thing as God's willing that we should be happy.[8] But, when an identification is intended as an explanation, there are two ways of taking it. Someone who says that being F is one and the same thing as being G may be attempting to explain what is to be F in terms of our prior understanding of what it is to be G; or he may be attempting to explain what is to be G in terms of our prior understanding of what it is to be F. So, in so far as the divine will theory is being put forward as an explanation, there are two ways of understanding the identification it makes. One can understand it as providing an explanation of the nature of basic facts about goodness in terms of God's will. For example, one can understand it as explaining what is it for it to be good that we should be happy in terms of God's willing that we should be happy. Now, *that* gives rise to the problems which I have been describing; and, fundamentally, to the problem that, whereas the basic facts about goodness seem to be necessary, it is hard, as we have seen, to understand how God's willing what he does could be necessary—hard, that is, if we are not allowed to appeal to the idea that he wills what he wills *because* it is good. But one could instead understand the identification as an explanation of the nature of God's will in terms of basic facts about goodness. For God to will that something should be so *is* for it to be a basic fact that it is good

---

[8] I sometimes talk of God's willing that we should be happy (say) as being one and the same thing as its being good that we should be happy (assuming that it is a basic fact that this is good); but I also sometimes talk of the fact that God wills that we should be happy as being one and the same fact as the fact that it is good that we should be happy; and I also sometimes talk of God's willing that we should be happy as being one and the same thing as its being a basic fact that it is good that we should be happy; and so on. I do so because it is often convenient to talk in terms of facts. But, if there is any doubt about what I mean when I talk in terms of facts, it should be understood in terms of the first way of putting things.

that that should be so. For God to will that we should be happy *is* for
it to be a basic fact that it is good that we should be happy. That is
how we are to understand what God's will is. And, of course, if we
take the identification *that* way, there is no longer a problem about
how it could be a necessary truth that God wills what he wills. Since
the basic fact that such-and-such is good is necessary, to understand
how God's willing that thing could be necessary is just to understand
that it is a basic fact that it is good.

So, here is an answer. But is it a satisfactory answer? Is it really an
explanation of what it is for God to will something, rather than
merely the invitation to use the words, 'God wills that . . .', to mean,
*It is good that . . .*? Does the proposal have anything to do with anything else that one might ordinarily understand by 'God'? I shall contend that it does.

## The Abstract Conception of God

We started the chapter with the view that the world exists because it
is good that it should. Suppose that we were to adopt the idea that
God's willing something was to be identified with its being a basic
fact that that thing is good. In that case, the view that the world exists
because it is good that there should be such a world becomes the view
that the world exists because God wills that it should. That is to say,
God is its creator. So, to propose that God's willing something is to
be identified with that thing's being good is not to offer an account
of the meaning of 'God wills . . .' which has nothing to do with any
ordinary conception of God. On the contrary, it is a central element
in many conceptions of God that he is the creator. So the suggestion
of how to understand the nature of God's will should not be con-
strued as being a suggestion for a new use of words, but rather as the
beginning of an account of a conception of *God*.

We have, I am suggesting, the beginning of a conception of God.
It is, indeed, an *abstract* conception: abstract in the sense that when
God is conceived of as willing something this is just identified with
the fact that that thing is good; and when God is conceived of as cre-

ating the world, this is just a matter of God's will being responsible for the existence of the world; that is to say, it is just a matter of the world's existing because it is good that it should. It is not a conception of a concrete *something* which wills and creates. But an abstract conception need not be an impoverished concept. In the remainder of this chapter I shall consider the extent to which our abstract conception of God might be enriched. I shall argue that it can be enriched in ways which will allow God to be characterized in many of the ways in which he can be characterized when conceived more concretely.

### Could God Act in the World?

The belief in God which I have described is, of course, a belief in a God who can act. It is the belief that he created the world. But can any other actions be ascribed to God—that is to say, does it make *sense* to ascribe any other actions to him, and in particular actions *in* the world which he has created? The answer is that there is no difficulty about this. As a first approximation we can say that God has acted in the world whenever it is true that some particular thing happens in the world because it is good that it should happen. But this is only a first approximation, because there are two types of case where it would be true that something has happened because it is good that it should, where, however, we might think that this did not amount to God's acting in the world. The first type of case is where people do things because of their knowledge of what is good. The second type of case is where what happens does so, indeed, because it is good that it should, but it is brought about because of the way the world was created. In both cases it might be thought that what happens is too indirectly connected with the goodness of it to constitute God's acting in the world. But it is easy enough to take care of this. We can say instead that we have a case of God's acting in the world whenever something happens in the world *directly* because it is good. But could such a thing happen? It is not at all obvious why not. Given that things can be *indirectly* brought about because of facts about goodness, it is surely possible for things to be brought about *directly* because they are good. There is just a slight worry, which does not have anything to do with the logical possibility that such a thing should happen; it is rather to do with the question of *why* God should need to intervene. Put in traditional terms, the worry is that God should not need to intervene in the workings of the world, because he could always have set things up at the creation so that the good thing would happen. He should not need to tinker with the world now. I shall return to this question in Chapter 7, when I shall discuss the question of whether we could have a good reason to suppose that God actually has acted in the world. But meanwhile it seems evident that, *if* there is going to be a reason for God to act in the world, it is going to be because there is a reason for God to *react* to something that happens in the world. So at this stage I shall ask merely whether, on the account I am offering, God *could* react to events in the world.

### Could God React to the World?

Can we explain what it would be for God to react to the world when abstractly conceived? There is no great difficulty. God's action occurs when something comes about in the world directly because it is good that it should. What will make it a *reaction*, to Peter's prayer, say? It will be a reaction if it happens *because of* Peter's prayer, because the prayer makes a difference to what would be good in the actual circumstances. Notice, by the way, that it must occur because of the prayer. It will be easiest to see this if we revert to the traditional terms. Supposing that God had in fact known that Peter was going to pray as he did, because he knew what the circumstances were going to be, and he knew that Peter was bound to make this prayer in those circumstances. In that case he would have been able to decide in advance of the prayer to bring about such-and-such a thing. That this thing would be good would depend on the fact that the prayer was going to take place, but God's decision would not be a *reaction* to the prayer. It would be a decision taken in anticipation of the prayer, not because of the prayer. (Of course, this possibility would not arise if

Peter's prayer were the outcome of free choice; for, in that case, he would not have been bound to make the prayer in the circumstances.) Avoiding these traditional terms, we can put it as follows. Suppose that the circumstances made the prayer inevitable, and so made it inevitable that it would be good for the thing in question to happen; and suppose that it was just for *these* reasons that the thing happened—that it was these things that led to its happening, not the prayer itself. Then what happened would not have been a *reaction* to the prayer, because it would not have happened *because* of the prayer, but rather because of the circumstances which made the prayer inevitable. (Much as the car does not stop because of the petrol gauge's registering empty, but because of the lack of petrol.)

So the position is this. We will have a case of God's reacting to Peter's prayer if the fact that he prays as he does makes it good that something should happen, and the thing happens because of the prayer, and because it is good that the thing in question should happen—*directly* because of this: that is, not because there is a law that this sort of thing should happen when a prayer like this is made; and not because one of us has brought the things about because we have seen that it would be good.

Let me emphasize two related things. The first is this. I have said that, in the case of God's reacting to a prayer, what happens will not happen because there is a law that, in cases of this sort, this sort of thing happens (and the law is as it is because it is good that it should be so). If that were the case we would not have a reaction by God. But we would *also* not expect what happens to happen because of a law that such things happen *when it is good that they should happen*. This is not because, if that were so, we should not have a case of God's reacting, but because his reacting would be determined by a law. And we should not expect this in the case of his acting in the world, any more than we would expect it in the case of the creation. This lack of a law determining when he acts corresponds to the freedom which is commonly attributed to God's actions when he is thought of more concretely. The second related point is that what I am describing as God's will should not be confused with God's *decision*. So if things that would be good do not happen, that is not because of the impotence of his decision. It is rather because he does not bring about everything which he wills should be so. One could, if one wished, speak of what God desires, instead of what he wills; but it is common enough for God's will to be spoken of in this way: to say, for instance, that God wills that we should not do wrong, but does not prevent our doing so.

I conclude, then, that there is no difficulty in the idea that God, conceived in the abstract way, could react to what happens in the world.

## Could God Know?

In describing how a reaction by God might be possible on the abstract conception, I did not say anything about God's knowing anything. *Could* he be thought of as knowing anything?

Well, at least in the context of an action by him there is no great difficulty. If he reacts to a certain feature of the world, it will be natural to think of him as having knowledge of that feature of the world.[9] That is to say, if something happens because it is good that it should happen, we can attribute to God knowledge of those things that contributed to the fact that it was good that the thing should happen. But in that case it will also be natural to attribute to him knowledge of all those things which have a bearing on whether it would be good that something should happen, whether or not the thing in fact happens because it is good that it should. That is to say, God's knowledge can be conceived of as extending at least to all those facts which have any bearing on whether it would be good that something should happen, or should be the case. And, if that amounts to everything whatsoever, God may be conceived of as omniscient.

---

[9]  Just as, in our case, it is by way of our beliefs about the world (and, when things go well, our knowledge of the world) that the way the world is combines with our willing of the good to produce intentional actions. See the penultimate paragraph of this chapter.

### A God who is Loving?

An important feature, *the* important feature, in many people's conception of God is that he is loving. He loves his creatures. Could God be thought of in this way on the abstract conception?

I take it that the central idea in the conception of God as loving is the idea that he cares about the welfare of his creatures, he wills what is good for them. And is not this idea immediately available on the abstract conception? Well, we need to be a little careful. Up to now we have been thinking of God's willing such-and-such as being identical with the basic fact that such-and-such is good. So he can will what would be good for Mary in a *general* sense. He can will what would be good for anyone like Mary, in circumstances like Mary's. That is to say, he wills a thing if it is a *necessary* truth that such a thing is good. But that is not, so far, to will *Mary's* good; it is not to love *Mary*. To do that it would have to be the case that he willed that such-and-such was true of Mary. And that would seem to be a matter of its being good that such-and-such was true of Mary. But that will be a contingent truth, depending as it does on what else is true of Mary, and what the circumstances are. But there is no great problem here. If we conceive of God as willing what is basically good, and also as having knowledge of those things that have a bearing on whether something would be *actually* good, it seems natural to conceive of him as also willing those things that would be actually good. So we can conceive of him, not only as willing what would be good for anyone like Mary, but also as willing, in particular, Mary's good. We can conceive of him as loving Mary.

How much is left out on this account? Certainly I have said nothing about *feelings*. And it is difficult to see how there could be room to ascribe feelings to God on the abstract conception, except to the extent that the ascription could be cashed out in terms of will, knowledge, and action. But this may not be thought to be a great loss. Even when we talk in traditional terms, the ascription to God of anger, or sadness, or amusement (for instance) may easily seem not to be literal, at any rate in so far as they are thought of literally as involving feelings.

## Could God Speak?

There are, no doubt, some interesting questions to be asked about the extent to which there could be a very close analogy between the way in which we use language and the way in which God might, whether we conceive of him in traditional terms or not.[10] But I shall largely ignore these questions, and concentrate rather on some things that may be achieved by speech—informing, promising, commanding. Could God do these things?

## Could God Inform?

Informing is fairly straightforward. The main requirement, if I am to inform you of something, is that I should create a suitable belief in you. It is true that not *any* old means by which I might deliberately create a belief in you will count as informing. I might start running in order to create in you the belief that I am in a hurry; but that would not be a case of *informing* you that I am in a hurry. There are at least two reasons for this. The first is that I will only strictly speaking be informing you if I use conventional means of some sort—typically, linguistic means of some sort. But, as I said, I am not going to pursue this. The second is that, when you learn that I am in a hurry because I am running, you *infer* that I am in a hurry from my behaviour. But when I inform you of something, you do not (at any rate consciously) infer whatever it is from my behaviour. Of course, you *could* acquire a belief by inference from my behaviour. You could think to yourself, 'He says that it is raining; so, he believes that it is raining; so it *is* raining.' But, if that is the way you acquire the belief that it is raining, I have not informed you of the fact. I imagine, then, that we will have come close enough to saying that God can inform,

---

[10] For a detailed and penetrating discussion see Nicholas Wolterstorff, *Divine Discourse: Philosophical Reflections on the Claim that God Speaks* (New York: Cambridge University Press, 1995).

if we can say that it is possible for him to create beliefs in people without relying on their making inferences. And there does not seem to be any problem of principle here. We shall have what we want if it is possible that a person may come to believe something more or less directly because it is good that he should believe it. *Perhaps* a little more is needed. Perhaps, just as in the normal case, when I inform you of something, you are aware of the means by which you are brought to have the belief, so in the case where a person is informed of something by God, he will need to be aware of the means by which he acquires his belief. That condition might be harder to satisfy in practice, though it is not clear that it raises problems of principle. Even in a case where there was nothing like a voice, or a sign—where, perhaps, it was simply a matter of the direct causing of a belief in a person—it would presumably be possible in principle for him to be aware that it was God who was responsible: that is to say, that the belief had arisen because it was good that it should. Though it would, of course, be important that the person could distinguish between the case where God was responsible for the belief, and the case where the belief arose from wishful thinking.

## Could God Promise?

Promises are a little trickier. It is true that normally, when you promise me that you will do something in suitable circumstances, I will believe that you will do it in those circumstances. Not quite always. I may think that you will be unable to, or are lying, or that something will crop up which will mean that you ought, after all, to break your promise. But we need not be concerned with these problems if it is God doing the promising. And, if the crucial thing about promising were simply the creation of a belief about how the promisor would act, there would be no problem. If God can create beliefs in general in people, there is no particular problem in the idea that he may create in them the belief that he will do something in certain circumstances. But it is not quite as simple as that. There is more to promising than creating a belief—otherwise there would be no

difference between the position of the promisee and the position of
someone who heard the promise being made. The additional crucial
element in a promise is that the promisor creates in the promisee a
right which he did not have before, a right to determine how the
promisee should behave in a certain area. If you promise me that you
will do something in certain circumstances, and those circumstances
arise, I can hold you to your promise (within certain limits), or I can
release you from it. The position is something like this, at least when
all goes well. In advance of making the promise you would be free to
determine for yourself what to do out of a range of acceptable
things—in particular, say, to pay me five pounds on Tuesday or to do
something else with the money. However, if you promise me that you
will pay me five pounds on Tuesday, then it is up to *me* whether you
pay me or not. Of course things may not go so well. In particular, it
may be that, as things turn out, paying me five pounds on Tuesday is
not an acceptable thing for you to do (even given my expectations and
those of others). In which case, it is not after all up to me whether you
pay me; nor would you have been free to choose that course of action
in those circumstances, if it had *not* been for the promise. It may even
have been the case that you should never have promised, because you
knew, or should have known, that paying me was not going to be an
acceptable course of action—perhaps it was not even your five
pounds. But again we can ignore these problems if it is God doing the
promising.

The question remains whether we can give any content to the idea
that God can transfer to me the right to determine how he should act
in certain circumstances. It may, it must be said, not be *that* important whether God can do this. It may be that, in so far as people are
interested in whether God can make promises, they are really only
interested in the question of whether he can bring it about that they
may be confident that he will act in a certain way. And about that
there seems to be no great difficulty. But in fact I think that it is possible to see how there is room for divine promises in the narrower
sense. Suppose that God were to offer me something, which I was free
to accept or not to accept. That would seem to amount to his giving
me the right to determine what he does; and it seems to be a possibility which is perfectly intelligible if one thinks of God in traditional

terms. But is it also intelligible if one is thinking of God along the lines I am proposing? Surely it is. To understand what it would be for God to offer me something, we just have to understand what it would be for God to react to a choice of mine, and what it would be for God to bring it about that I have such a choice. And there seems to be no special difficulty about that.

## Could God Command?

God is often thought of as issuing commands to his creatures. The commands may be general, may be thought of as the issuing of a moral law; or they may be particular, as when some person is told to do some particular thing. Is there room for this sort of conception on the abstract account?

A command properly speaking involves language. To command someone to do something is to *tell* him to do something. And, where the commander has the authority to command the person to do a certain thing, the very fact that he has given the command means that the person ought do what he has been told to do—at any rate, other things being equal. So, to think of God as commanding would, strictly speaking, involve thinking of him as speaking, or using some other linguistic device. No doubt there is no insuperable difficulty about this in so far as God is traditionally conceived. And, of course, he will be thought of as having the authority to command; so, the very fact that he commands me to do something will mean that I ought to do it. But how does the abstract conception fare? Well, even if there is a problem about ascribing *speech* to him, we know that there is no problem about thinking of him as *willing*. His willing that something should occur is simply its being good that that thing should occur. What is more, the very fact that God wills that I should do something means, of course, that I should do it; for to say this is just to say that the very fact that it would be good that I do it means that I should do it. So, even if we cannot think of God as strictly speaking commanding me on the abstract conception, we can think of his relationship to me as being somewhat similar. Would anything important be lost, if we cannot think of God's commanding in some rather stricter sense? I shall argue in the next section that it would not.

### Divine Commands and Duty

I mentioned earlier in the chapter, when discussing the idea that God was the source of moral value, that there was a view that, though God was not responsible for the existence of value in general, he *was* responsible for the existence of moral duties.

Now, it does seem quite plausible to distinguish between those things which it would be good to do, and those things which we have a moral duty to do; between those things which it would have been good to do, and those things which we were wrong not to do. It would be good if we could act like saints or heroes; but we have not failed in our moral duty if we do not. To act like saints or heroes is to go beyond the call of duty. To which some would add: it would be good if we made the most of our talents; but, in so far as others do not suffer if we do not, we shall not have done anything morally wrong if we fail. How is this distinction to be understood?

The view I mentioned is that the distinction, rightly understood, is a distinction between those good actions which God commands us to perform and those which he does not command. For, one might say, for an action to be my moral duty is for it to be *required* of me. But by whom? It cannot be by other *humans*. Their requirements may determine my legal duty, but not my moral duty. There could be no one with the appropriate authority but God.[11] However, if the distinction is to be made in terms of God's commands, it is evident that we shall need to attribute to God something more like commanding, properly understood. God's *willing*, as it is understood on the abstract account, will obviously not be enough, because he wills *all*

---

[11] John Mackie describes (but, of course, does not subscribe to) such a line of thought. See his *The Miracle of Theism* (Oxford: Clarendon Press, 1982), 102.

things which it would be good that we should do; not just *some* of them, those that constitute our duties.

So must we find room for the idea that there are divine commands properly speaking, if we are to make sense of the distinction between what is good and what is our duty? I shall argue that there is no such need. In so far as we can explain the distinction in terms of divine commands, we can equally well explain it without any such appeal—at least, we can if the distinction is an important one.

Let us ask *why* God might command us to do some good things but not others. There are two sorts of account according to which his choice of what to command would be *arbitrary*. I think that both should be rejected.

The first account is easily dealt with. It says that God commands some things rather than others, not because he thinks it *better* to command this rather than that, but simply because he *prefers* to. The objection to this account is not so much that, if it were true, we should have no obligation to *do* what was commanded. We might, after all, agree that it was all right for parents to tell a child to do something just because they liked the idea. And we might think that, as long as what the child was told to do was not wrong, or unduly burdensome, the child would have an obligation to do what he was told. Similarly (or *a fortiori*) we would have an obligation to obey our creator.[12] The objection rather is that it does not seem attractive to attribute to God *this* sort of arbitrary preference; this *fancying* of one thing rather than another, without any reason.

The second account is a little more promising, perhaps. According to this account there is something good *in itself* about our obeying commands given by God (because he is our creator, perhaps); something good about obeying such commands independently of their content, or at least in addition to it. That being the case, it is a good thing that God should command us to do some things, even if they are already things which it would be good to do, because, if we do them, *more* good will have come about than if we had done them without any such command. The account would perhaps go on to say that it would not be a good thing for God to command us to do

[12] For this comparison see Swinburne, *The Coherence of Theism*, 205–6.

*everything* good that we could possibly do—because, perhaps, this
would be too burdensome. That being so, it may be the case that his
commanding this rather than that is just arbitrary. So, according to
the account, he has a reason for commanding *something*; but no reason to command this rather than that.

But can we *really* accept this; that there is something good about
the mere obedience to a command, where the command has been
given for the sole purpose of giving us the opportunity to obey it? I
think that, in so far as we are tempted to think that there is something good about mere obedience, it is probably because we are con-
fusing what is envisaged with something else. We may think that mere
obedience is a good thing in so far as it manifests trust that the person commanding knows best. But the good involved in that case is
the good of *trust*, not the good of obedience. And it is not what is
envisaged in the present account. That account does not envisage our
trusting God to know what is best, and our obeying him because we
think that his command is given on the basis of that knowledge of
what is best. On the contrary: the account envisages that he may have
no such reason; so, in so far as we are not deceived, our obedience
will not be based on any such trust. Again, we may confuse obedience with the surrendering of our wills to God, where this would
involve ceasing to decide for ourselves what we should do, and letting
God himself determine our will directly. Perhaps this would be a
good thing; perhaps not. But the important thing in the present context is to notice two things. The first is that we could make sense of
this idea on the abstract conception of God. To surrender my will to
God would be a matter of my allowing my will to be determined
directly by facts about what it would be good for me to will, rather
than as result of any use of my reason. The second thing we should
notice is that this surrendering of one's will is quite different from
what the present account envisages. To surrender one's will is to cease
to act on the basis of what one thinks one ought to do. The present
account, on the other hand, envisages that we continue to act on the
basis of what we think we ought to do, but that we attach weight to
the mere fact that to do so would be to obey God's (arbitrary) command.

Suppose, then, that we assume (for the purposes of this divine command theory of duty) that God has some *reason* for commanding this good thing rather than that. What reason could he have?

Now, there are various reasons why it might be good for there to be commands which we can dismiss as irrelevant for our present purposes. One such reason has to do with the usefulness of the obeying of commands where there is a need for coordination. This is one of the reasons for having coxes in boats, or captains in football teams. It is also a reason for having laws about which side of the road to drive on. The last example is a particularly pure one. It does not matter *which* side of the road we drive on, as long as we agree; but without some rule our behaviour is unlikely to be coordinated. Conceivably it might be important that God should give commands to enable coordination. It is not quite clear why he should, since the same end could be achieved by two other means. The first would be if we were to come to see that coordination in a particular area was important, and we ourselves agreed on the laws—in other words, if we were to do the sort of thing we do to some extent anyway. The second would be if we had appropriate natural preferences to act in one way rather than another. But whether he might give commands for such a reason or not, commands given for reasons of this sort could not explain the distinction in question. This is simply because some obvious cases where we commonly take ourselves to have moral duties do not fit this profile. Most people, in so far as they think that they have moral duties at all, would think that they have a duty not to cause others to suffer unnecessarily. But this is not a matter of something which is important because of a need for coordination; there is no hint of *arbitrariness* about it—that is to say, it is not a matter of there being various alternatives which would have done more or less as well. On the contrary: not causing others to suffer seems to be something which is *naturally* of the greatest importance; its importance does not lie in the fact that *it* happens to have been commanded, rather than something else. And I take it that it will not do to reply that God creates in us the *illusion* that it is so important in this way, in order to secure coordination of behaviour. Apart from the fact that this reply would seem to attribute deception to God, it could hardly be well motivated, unless it can be shown that to abandon this intuition of a lack of arbitrariness in this case would be the only way of preserving more powerful intuitions about the distinction between moral duties and other things it would be good that we should do. But we have certainly not reached *that* stage.

For similar reasons, we can dismiss as irrelevant another way in which commands may be useful. They may be useful because people's judgements in a certain area may be too unreliable. So it is best to *tell* them what to do, rather than letting them decide for themselves what they ought to do. But this does not fit the case of not causing unnecessary suffering. Here, if anywhere, we do not seem to be in any doubt; and not because we are in no doubt that we are *commanded* not to cause unnecessary suffering, but because we are in no doubt that it is wrong in itself.

What I have said about these irrelevant reasons for commanding, suggests a rather more plausible account of why God might command us to do the sorts of thing we regard as our moral duties. He might command us to do them because it was particularly *important* that we should. Perhaps the reason might be that this sort of action was particularly important for human welfare. Or perhaps it might be that this action would be *relatively* easy for ordinary people to do, so that (perhaps) they would normally be blameworthy if they did not perform the action in the appropriate circumstances. Or perhaps it might be for a combination of these reasons. But in *that* case there seem to be two powerful objections to the account of the distinction given by divine command theory. The first objection is that, if there were *already* an important difference between the sorts of things we have a duty to do, and the sorts of things it would be merely good to do, it is not clear why God *should* command us to do the former. They would have particular importance even without his commanding them. Does God command them in order to give them *more* importance than they would naturally have? But why should he do that? And the second objection is that there would immediately be an alternative account of the distinction. Instead of saying that we have a duty to do this thing because God commanded it, and he commanded it because it is an action which is of particular importance for human welfare and so on, we can say that we have a duty to do it just because it is an action which is of particular importance for human welfare and so on. That is to say, duties could be distinguished from other good actions by just those features which, on the divine command theory, constitute God's reasons for commanding the actions.

Perhaps it may be thought that this answer is not adequate; perhaps it may be thought that, even if the features involved explain why some actions are duties while others are not, they do not *constitute* the difference between being a duty and not being a duty. The difference could only be constituted by the fact of God's command. I am not sure what the basis for this view might be. But I think that we can reply as follows. The primary reason for being interested in the distinction is because there is thought to be an important difference between things that are our moral duties and things that are not. If we can point to an important difference, and, what is more, this is the difference which, on the divine command theory, constitutes God's reason for commanding the things that are our duties, then we do not need to appeal to any command of God's in order to explain why these things are of particular importance. That being the case, even if this difference does not *constitute* the difference between duties and other things, and even if, for something to be a duty, it really would have to be commanded by God, we shall not have lost anything which matters if, on the abstract conception, there is no room for ascribing commands strictly speaking to God. Perhaps (*perhaps*) the important difference will not be properly marked by saying that we have a *duty* to do these things. But that will not alter the fact that it is particularly important that we do them.

### The Adequacy of the Abstract Conception

In this chapter I have been developing an abstract conception of God. I have claimed that it is a conception that allows in particular for the possibility of God's willing, God's knowing, and God's acting and reacting. What I have said does amount to the claim that he *does* will—he wills whatever is good; it also amounts to the claim that he *does* know—he knows all those things that are relevant to whether something would be good. I am not, however, claiming that he *does* act, beyond claiming that he is the creator of the world; in particular I am not claiming that he reacts to particular things in the world. My claim is only that the abstract conception is rich enough to make this possible. But is the abstract conception rich enough? Does it fail to make room for some important attribute of God's? Well, what is important to one person may not be important to another. So I will not try to answer that question. I will however consider two objections. The first is that on the abstract account God is not a *person*; and the second is that what the abstract account represents as God's willing, knowing, and acting, are not *really* cases of willing, knowing, and acting at all. So to use those words is just sophistry.

Now it indeed true that, on the abstract conception, God is not a person. This is not because he is something *other* than a person; it is because, on the abstract conception, God is not a *something* at all. That being the case it is, no doubt, also true that, on the abstract account, 'willing' and 'knowing' cannot have their ordinary senses. For, in their ordinary senses, it is, no doubt, the case that there cannot be any willing or knowing unless a person—or *something*—wills or knows. However, that does not mean that there cannot be enough similarities between the way God is described on the abstract account, and the way persons are, to make this way of describing God justifiable. And here, I think, there are two points to be made. The first is that, whatever else is true of persons, one outstanding feature of them is that they provide an interface between goodness and the world. It is by way of them, and perhaps only by way of them in our experience, that what is good comes to affect the way the world is. And it is by way of their knowledge (when things go well) and their will that this comes about. That being so, it is not wholly inappropriate to use this language, albeit by way of analogy, to describe what happens when what is good affects the way things are directly. The second point concerns the conception of God as a person. To the extent that he is thought of as a person, it will be easier to apply the terms 'will' and 'know' to him literally. But for all that, in doing so, we will at most have an understanding of the *function* of his knowledge and his will in so far as it provides a route from facts about goodness and facts about the world to those facts about the world that arise by his action.[13] We will not, surely, have any understanding of the intrinsic nature of God's knowing or willing or acting; and we will not have any understanding of the intrinsic nature of his personhood. Indeed, to the extent that he is thought of as outside time and space, the model of human knowing and willing and human personhood can hardly provide so much as a hint. That being the case, it does not seem that we will lose much of importance if, instead of a conception of God according to which the route from facts about goodness and facts about the world to further facts about the world involves something of an unknown nature performing operations of an unknown nature—if, instead of *that* conception, we have a conception of God which involves no more than the route.

I have defended in this chapter an abstract conception of God according to which it is possible for God to will, to know, to act, and to react; a conception, moreover, on which God's will is intimately connected with morality. And, taking this chapter with what has gone before, I have defended a *belief* in a God who wills what is good, who is the creator of the world, who has knowledge of the world, and who loves us. And this I take to constitute the central core of many people's belief in God.

---

[13] William Alston emphasizes the importance of function for the understanding of mental predicates as applied to God. See his 'Functionalism and Theological Language' (Ithaca, N.Y.: Cornell University Press, 1989); first published in *American Philosophical Quarterly* 22 (1985), 221–30.

# 6

# The Problem of Evil

I HAVE SUGGESTED that we can explain the existence of a world such as this by supposing that it exists because it is good that there should be such a world. There is an obvious problem about this. It seems to be an undoubted fact that there are bad things about the world, that there are evils in it. How is this compatible with the claim that it exists because it is good that it should? To raise this question is to raise the problem of evil.

The traditional problem of evil is this. How could a God who is omnipotent, omniscient, and perfectly good allow there to be evil? If he is omniscient he would know about any possible evil; if he is omnipotent he would be able to prevent it; if he is perfectly good he would wish to prevent it.[1] And not just, how could a God such as this allow there to be *some* evil; but, how could a God such as this allow there to be so *much* evil?

## Omnipotence and Omniscience

The traditional problem makes use of two notions that are rather difficult to define in any satisfactory manner: omnipotence and omniscience. Fortunately, for the purposes of our discussion we do not need to be too precise. For our purposes it will be enough if we sup-

---

[1] As Hume's Philo puts it, 'Is he willing to prevent evil, but not able? then he is impotent. Is he able, but not willing? then he is malevolent. Is he both able and willing? whence then is evil?' David Hume, *Dialogues Concerning Natural Religion* (first published 1779), ed. R. H. Popkin (Indianapolis, Ind.: Hackett, 1980), 63.

pose that to attribute omniscience to God is to attribute to him knowledge of everything he could in principle know, and not, of course, knowledge of what he could not in principle know. And again, for our purposes, it will be enough to note that to attribute omnipotence to God is *not* to attribute to him the power to do what is metaphysically impossible, but is, of course, amongst other things, to attribute to him the power to create, not only things, but laws of nature.

### Appeals to Ignorance

One sort of response to the problem of evil is to plead ignorance; or at least the fallibility of human reason. This might take various forms. One form might be like this. One might point to our possible ignorance of what is good and what is evil. With this in mind one might suggest that, even if the problem *seems* insoluble to us, that may be just because our conceptions of good and evil are inadequate. Perhaps, what seems evil to us is not *really* evil. There is an obvious difficulty about this response, however, if we want to appeal to the goodness of the world in explaining why a belief in God is reasonable. Of course, our beliefs about good and bad are fallible, as all our beliefs are. But we cannot have it both ways. We cannot simply put on one side those beliefs about evil which may embarrass us, while retaining those beliefs about good which suit us. So, at any rate, this response is not available in the context of the sort of claim I have been making about the reasonableness of belief in God.

Another form of the response might emphasize our ignorance of God's purposes.[2] One might say that, even if, from our narrow perspective, it seems that there is too much evil in the world to be compatible with the existence of a perfectly good, omniscient, omnipotent God, that is because we know so little about God's purposes. Although the good things we are aware of may not seem to explain the evils we are aware of, perhaps that is just because we are ignorant (and, one might add, too inclined to overestimate our own

---

[2] See Descartes, *Meditations on First Philosophy*, Fourth Meditation, 38–9.

importance in the great scheme of things). Perhaps, in particular, there are good things of which we have no conception, and those evil things have a crucial role to play in the coming to be of these good things. But this form of the response is also unsatisfactory. To start with, it could not be sufficient as it stands, because it does not address two worries one might have. In the first place one might worry about how it could *ever* be that evil was necessary for good to be possible. If it could never be necessary, goods that we do not know about could not explain the presence of evils we do know about. But, even if one could see how evil might be inevitable if certain good things were to be possible, and even if one could see how such good things might, in some cases, compensate for the inevitable evils, one might think that there were certain things which were so evil that they could not be explained in this way by *any* good. If this were one's worry, the present response would not do. But, quite apart from these shortcomings, this form of response suffers from a similar defect to the first form. *If* we are going to appeal to the goodness of the world in order to explain why a belief in God is reasonable, we must have a good reason *from our perspective* to believe that the world is indeed good. We cannot then respond to the problem of evil by conceding that from our perspective the world may not seem good. Of course, our perspective is fallible; but again we cannot have it both ways. We cannot rely on it for the purposes of providing reasons for a belief, and cast doubt on it for the purposes of defending the belief. So this appeal to ignorance and fallibility will not be satisfactory in this context.

## No Good Without Evil

It is sometimes suggested that evil is inevitable if there is to be good, just because there could be no such thing as good, if there were not such a thing as evil to provide a contrast.[3] It is, however, quite unobvious why anyone should suppose that this is true. Perhaps there is a

---

[3] John Mackie describes such a view. See his *The Miracle of Theism* (Oxford: Clarendon Press, 1982), 151.

confusion with the claim that if good is *possible*, evil must be *possible*. And perhaps that is plausible, if the possibility that is being talked of is a *metaphysical* possibility. But it does not imply that if good is *actual*, evil must be *actual*, or even inevitable. More likely there is a confusion with a different claim, that if we are to acquire the concept of goodness, we must encounter evil as well as good; somewhat as one might claim that if we are to acquire the concept of red we must come across other colours. One might indeed think that one could develop this idea to show how, in one particular case, it was impossible to have a certain good without evil. For one might claim that it is a *good* thing to possess the concept of good. And *this* good thing would not be possible without evil. But this would be an unimpressive argument. Even if we were to accept the claim that to have a concept of something it is necessary to encounter things which do not fit the concept, the argument would not work for two reasons. First, as far as this argument goes, a very small amount of trivial evil ought to be enough. So we would be in no position to explain the apparently great amount of untrivial evil in the world. Secondly, it ought to be enough for us to encounter things which were not good, but were not evil either—neutral things. And, what is more, that would be enough to allow us to have the concept of evil as well. We could construct that concept from the concept of good. Something is evil just if its absence would be good. So we ought to reject this account.

## Free Will

What is probably the most popular solution to the problem of evil appeals to the goodness of free will.[4] The account goes like this. We have free will in the sense that we can make choices which are not determined by laws of nature (including laws about the operations of

---

[4] See particularly Alvin Plantinga, *The Nature of Necessity* (Oxford: Clarendon Press, 1974), ch. IX, and Richard Swinburne, *The Existence of God* (Oxford: Clarendon Press, 1979), chs. 10 and 11, and his *Providence and the Problem of Evil* (Oxford: Clarendon Press, 1998), chs. 5, 7, and 8.

the mind). That is to say, in certain cases we make choices which are not rendered inevitable, given the laws of nature, by anything that precedes the choice. In some cases, what is more, we are in a position to make choices between things that are very evil and things that are not; between things that are very good and things that are not. And this ability is, furthermore, a very good thing. However, this account goes on, if this good thing is to exist, evil is inevitable, even great evil. It is not inevitable in the sense that it is *bound to occur*. It is inevitable in the sense that it would be impossible to ensure that it did not occur. God could indeed ensure that I do not bring about evil by making me choose good; but that would not be a *free* choice. He could also ensure that my choice of evil is always frustrated; but that would be at the expense of what is valuable about free will. What is valuable about it is not the bare power to choose things in the sense of just *willing* them. I have the power to *will* that I fly home and thus avoid traffic jams. But that power is quite worthless. What is valuable is the power to do, to choose successfully. So, to the extent that God frustrates my choices, he deprives me of what is good. And it is not only the *actual* frustrating of my choices that would deprive me of what is good. If God were always waiting in the wings, ready to frustrate me should I make an evil choice, he would have deprived me of freedom, even if I never made an evil choice. So God could not ensure that evil does not occur by intervening like this. But nor could he ensure that I did not do evil by constructing the laws of nature in such a way that the circumstances always prevented my choice of evil; because then, of course, I would not have the freedom to choose evil. So God could not have rendered evil impossible without rendering the freedom to choose evil impossible; that is to say, without making that good thing impossible.

## Is There Such a Thing as Free Will?

This account will work, of course, only if there is such a thing as free will. We seem to *think* that we have free will. But are there any reasons for thinking that we do not? I will discuss just three important reasons that might be advanced for saying that we do not.

The first reason appeals to another element of the way we think about our actions, and claims that it is incompatible with our having free will. It goes like this. We think that, when we make choices, we make them, generally, for *reasons*. But, if we make a choice for a reason, that means that it must have arisen from beliefs of ours, together perhaps with desires. But this means that our choice must have been *caused* by our beliefs.[5] And this means that our choice must have been *determined* by our beliefs together with other factors preceding the choice. So it was not free after all. So at any rate choices made for *reasons* are not free. So in so far as we have any free will, it consists simply in the power to make choices without reasons. And *that* is not very valuable. Is this a good argument? I do not think it is. In effect we have already considered the facts it appeals to in Chapter 4. There I used our beliefs about actions done for reasons precisely to argue that we should not think of all cases of causation, or all cases where one thing gives rise to another, as involving laws. The position is this. We appear to be confronted with three inconsistent propositions: that we make free choices for reasons; that choices made for reasons are caused by (or arise from) beliefs; that, if anything arises from something else, there must be a deterministic law connecting them. The argument which we are considering invites us to reject the first proposition (which we naturally believe) and accept the other two. But, given that there do not seem to be any very powerful arguments for the third proposition, we should, I suggest, retain our belief in the first two, and reject the third.

The second reason for thinking that we do not have free will appeals to another element in our ordinary thinking. We make *predictions* about how others will behave; and we think that these predictions are rational.[6] But, as I argued in Chapter 2, they would not be rational, if we thought that it was just a matter of chance that the

[5] See Donald Davidson, 'Actions, Reasons and Causes', in his *Essays on Actions and Events* (Oxford: Clarendon Press, 1980); first published in *Journal of Philosophy*, 60 (1963), 685–700.
[6] See Hume, *An Enquiry concerning Human Understanding*, sect. VIII, pt. I.

things on which we base our predictions were in fact often followed by the actions predicted. So, we must suppose that the actions must be connected by law with the things on which we base our predictions. But the most this shows is that there must be a *tendency* for the things that constitute our evidence to be followed by the actions predicted; it cannot be *simply* a matter of chance. But that does not mean that our actions must be connected with the basis for the predictions by *deterministic* laws. So the argument fails.

The third reason is a little like the second, except that it concerns explanation rather than prediction. We sometimes think that we can explain people's behaviour in terms of their environment in various ways. For instance we may think that we can explain this man's bad tempered behaviour towards his wife by the brain damage he suffered in a car accident. We think that we can explain this person's abusive behaviour in terms of the fact that he was himself abused as a child. But that seems to suggest that we think of the behaviour as determined by the state of the brain in the one case, or the early experiences in the other. And, the argument continues, although we are less inclined to explain *unproblematic* behaviour like this, we have just as much reason to. That is, we have just as much reason to regard all behaviour as determined. But this is not a very strong argument. It may indeed suggest that we do not pay enough attention to the role of the environment and physical state of the brain in affecting unproblematic behaviour; but it does not suggest that we ought to regard all behaviour as *determined* by such things, rather than just influenced by them.

## Could God Know How I Would choose?

The free will account, as I have presented it, suggests that God could not ensure that no evil was freely chosen. The reason is that to attempt to do so by interfering would mean that the choice was not, after all, *free*; and to attempt to do so by using suitable laws of nature to bring about suitable choices would also mean that the choices would not be free. Nonetheless, it might be claimed, there could *be* a

world in which free creatures never did wrong; there is no impossibility in *that*. And in that case there is no impossibility in God's creating a world in which free creatures never did wrong.[7] However, to
claim that would not be enough. Unless God could *know* how free
creatures would behave in all possible circumstances (or, at any rate,
a very wide range of possible circumstances), he would not be in a
position to *ensure* that he created a world in which no free creatures
did anything wrong. At best, he could manipulate the *likelihood* of
wrongdoing. So, for God to ensure the absence of wrong, he would
have to know such things as that, if Eve were tempted in such and
such circumstances, she would choose to eat the apple. One should
notice, by the way, that it would not be enough for God to know
about all people's *actual* free choices. In deciding what sort of world
to create he would need to know what *would* happen if the world were
to be like *this*, and what *would* happen if it were to be like *that*. And
that would mean knowing how people would behave in circumstances which will never actually arise; knowing, indeed, how people
who will never exist would have behaved.

Is such knowledge possible?[8] Well it is obvious that there could
not be any knowledge of how free creatures would choose, if there
were no such facts about how they would choose. Indeed, on the
abstract conception of God, the question of whether he could have
such knowledge is effectively the same as the question of whether
there are any such facts. For, on that conception, God knows any
facts that have any bearing on whether something would be good;
and surely, if there were facts as how free creatures would choose,
they would have such a bearing. So, are there any such facts? It is not
at all clear that there are. One needs to remember that, on this picture, it is being assumed that a person's choices—*my* choices, say—
are free in the sense of not being determined by laws. And the sort of
facts we are talking about are facts about how I *would* behave, or
would have behaved. Not how I very *probably* would have behaved.

---

[7] See Mackie, *The Miracle of Theism*, 164–6.

[8] Luis de Molina (1535–1600) thought it was possible, and called it 'middle know-
ledge'. See his *On Divine Foreknowledge (Part IV of the Concordia)*, trans. Alfred J.
Freddoso (Ithaca, N.Y.: Cornell University Press, 1988), Disputation 52. See also
Plantinga, *The Nature of Necessity*, ch. IX.

To see the problem, consider the following example. (So as to avoid distraction by extraneous features, I have chosen an example which does not involve choice at all.) Suppose a coin is tossed, and it comes down heads. And suppose that the nature of the coin, together with the way in which it was tossed and the surrounding circumstances, did not determine that it would come down heads. It *could* have come down tails, but did not. Suppose further that the coin is never tossed again. Now, let us ask the following questions: first, 'Is it the case that, *if* the coin had been tossed a second time, and the nature of the coin, the method of tossing, and the relevant circumstances had been the same, it would have come down heads?'; second, 'Is it the case that, if the coin had been tossed a second time, and the nature of the coin, the method of tossing, and the relevant circumstances had been the same, it would have come down tails?' The most plausible answer seems to be that it *might* have come down heads, and it *might* have come down tails; but it is not true that it *would* have come down heads, and it is not true that it *would* have come down tails. But if it is the most plausible answer in the case of the coin, it is, surely, also the most plausible answer in the case of questions about how *I* would have behaved in certain hypothetical circumstances. As long as my choice is thought of as not determined, it will not be true that I *would* have done this, nor true that I *would* have done that. At most it will be true that it was very *likely*, even overwhelmingly *likely*, that I would have done this rather than that.

Actually there is rather a strong reason to suppose that, even if there were such facts about how I would behave, they would not be facts about how I would *freely* choose.[9] But in that case, to suppose that there are such facts in the case of every piece of behaviour is to suppose that there is no free will after all. The reason is this. Consider the case where my behaviour is determined by laws. In that case my behaviour, it is natural to think, would not be free. Why not? The reason, surely, is that my behaviour would then be necessitated by factors for which I was not responsible—the laws of nature and the circumstances which, together with the laws, determined my

    [9] See William Hasker, *God, Time and Knowledge* (Ithaca, N.Y.: Cornell University Press, 1989), 39–52.

behaviour. Of course, one might think that I could have been responsible for some of the circumstances. But any choice I made will, on
this picture, have been determined, in its turn, by prior circumstances,
and so on. Eventually we will get back to circumstances that preceded
my birth. Now consider the case where there is no *law* determining
that I choose this action in these circumstances, but it is nonetheless
true that, if those circumstances were to arise, I would choose that
action. The crucial question is whether *I* could be responsible for this
hypothetical fact. How could I be? Perhaps I might be if those circumstances did actually arise, and I chose the action. Perhaps by
choosing the action I would be responsible for the fact. But this could
not be so, if God *made use of the fact* in deciding whether to create a
world in which those circumstances would arise.[10] The reason is that
my choice must have depended on some features of the circumstances
(at the very least the circumstance that I existed); and they, in their
turn, will have depended on God's decision, which will have
depended on his knowledge of the hypothetical fact. But, in that case,
this hypothetical fact could not *itself* have depended on my choice. If
the choice depended on the circumstances, which depended on God's
decision, which depended on the hypothetical fact, *it* cannot have
depended on my choice. And it will not much help to suggest that the
hypothetical fact depended on some *other* choice of mine. That will
just put off the evil day. For the question will arise whether I could
have been responsible for the hypothetical fact that I would make *that*
choice in *those* circumstances. So it seems that, if God is going to
make use of these hypothetical facts about my choices in deciding
what world to create, *I* cannot be responsible for them. But, in that
case, my choice *will* be the necessary outcome of things for which I

---

[10] Notice that the fact that God has knowledge of something, on the abstract conception, does not necessarily mean that he can act on this knowledge to produce a
certain outcome. For instance, the fact that I am going to choose something freely
tomorrow may mean that it would be good that something should happen today. But,
if God were to act on his knowledge of my choice to bring something about today, that
would mean that my choice tomorrow had given rise to something today. And, if one
thinks (as I do not, in fact) that it is metaphysically impossible for a later thing to give
rise to an earlier thing, one will think that my choice could not have had such an effect.
Would that mean that God was not omnipotent? Of course not. An omnipotent being
is not required to be able to do the metaphysically impossible.

am not responsible—the hypothetical facts and the circumstances. So
I shall be no more free than if my behaviour had been determined by
laws.

It is worth considering whether the free will defence would be
undermined, if, contrary to what I have argued, it were to be conceded that there are facts about how free creatures would behave and
would have behaved, and that enough of them were available to God
for him to make use of when deciding what sort of world to create.
Some people have thought that the free will defence could survive this
concession.[11] It might survive, they have suggested, because it
remains possible that, although there is no impossibility in there
*being* a world in which free creatures do no wrong, it was impossible
for God to create such a world. For consider this. It is evident that in
some of the actual circumstances that have arisen I have done something wrong. So, although there was no *impossibility* that I should do
right in those circumstances, it was *actually* the case that in some of
those circumstances I would do wrong. So, as long as God created a
world with those circumstances it was, as a matter of fact, going to
be the case that I would do some wrong. But what if he had created
a world in which different circumstances had obtained? Well, perhaps
the facts about how I would behave in various circumstances mean
that in *any* world in which I existed I would do some wrong—not as
a matter of necessity, but as a matter of fact. But what if he had created a world in which I did not exist? Well, perhaps the facts about
how *you* would have behaved, and the facts about how any *other* people, actual and possible, would have behaved, mean that *whatever*
world God had created, with *whatever* circumstances and *whatever*
people, there would have been *some* wrong, as long as there was freedom. In that case God *could not* have created a world with free creatures in which there was no wrong; although there could have *been*
such a world. So, on this account, we could explain how there could
be creatures who freely choose to do wrong, while allowing that God
decided to create the world in the knowledge that these creatures
would do wrong things in these circumstances.

<hr>

[11] See especially Plantinga, *The Nature of Necessity*, ch. IX.

But there is a problem about this account. The problem lies in the status of these hypothetical facts about how people would behave. They are not *necessary* truths; they could have been otherwise. As I have said, there is no impossibility about my never doing wrong. So, if they could have been otherwise, why could not God have *made* them otherwise, if he is omnipotent? Why should we think of his choice as being constrained by these facts? The obvious answer would be that if these facts *had* been determined by God, the choices would not have been free, because God would then have determined how people would behave. But the question is, *why* should it be that, if God had determined these facts, there would not have been freedom? Now there *is* a plausible answer. And the answer is that, if God had determined how I would behave in certain circumstances, that would mean that my behaviour would be the inevitable outcome of factors for which I was not responsible. However, if this plausible answer is to work, it will not help merely to say that God did not determine these facts, unless it is also claimed that *I* am responsible for the facts. Because, unless I am, my behaviour will *still* be the inevitable outcome of factors for which I am not responsible. So, if the present account is to succeed, it will have to do one of two things. Either it will have to explain how I can be responsible for these facts about how I would behave, in spite of the fact that they were available to God as a basis for his creative decisions. Or it will have to forgo the plausible explanation for why God's determination of the facts would be incompatible with my freedom; and it will have to provide a different explanation.

I conclude that it seems rather doubtful that the free will defence could survive the concession that God could have made his decision about what world to create on the basis of knowledge of how free creatures would choose.

## Evils That Are Not Intended

We think that we have free will. We may, of course, be wrong. And, if we *are* wrong, this attempt to show that some evils are inevitable

*God and Goodness*

will fail. I will say a little about this possibility later. But, even if we have free will, and even if the goodness of free will can explain why there should be *some* evils, it is not clear that it can explain all. One problematical category I shall come back to: lives which contain so much evil that it would have been better for the person if he had never been born. But there is another category to which I shall turn now.

The evils that the free will account by itself deals with are evils that are deliberately brought about by free choices. But there are also many evils that are not of this sort. There are evils which are the unintended and unexpected outcome of free choices; and there are evils in whose production free choice played no part. In fact, presumably, pretty well *all* evils that befall *human beings* are, in one way or another, the outcome of free choices—if only because it seems unlikely that there have ever been human beings whose existence did not depend on some choice at some stage made by their parents—at any rate if we ignore problems of chickens and eggs. So, let us consider first evils which are the unintended outcome of free choice. Could it be argued that evils of this sort, as well as intended evils, are inevitable if some good is to be achieved?

On the face of it, they are not inevitable. There seem to be two ways in which they might have been avoided. The first way would be if we had had more perfect knowledge than has in fact been the case. The second way would be if things had been so arranged that evils could not occur without evil intent. Might we have had more perfect knowledge? Well one possibility is this. God might have caused us to have appropriate true beliefs when it mattered, by constantly inserting such beliefs into us. But that perhaps that *would* involve a loss; for it seems likely that beliefs acquired in this way would not be rational. And rationality seems to be a *good* thing, and irrationality a bad thing. On the other hand, even if they would be irrational, and irrationality is a bad thing, it is not obvious that things as a whole would be worse if God intervened from time to time to save us from the most disastrous of our mistakes; if from time to time he caused us to have vital bits of information. Perhaps they would. Perhaps, in any case, there is something good about our being left, for the most part, to find our own way through the world—at least as far as ordinary facts are concerned. And, at the very least, it must be conceded that, if

God were to intervene in the way suggested at all frequently, our lives would be lives of a very different sort. But in any case there is another alternative. Surely God could have made us much better at acquiring information rationally. He could have given us superior methods of data acquisition (superior senses, perhaps), and could have given us better powers of theory construction, and so on. Of course, beings which were so good at knowing about the world would be very unlike us. And this, I shall be suggesting later, is an important consideration. But it does not mean, of course, that unintended evils could *not* be avoided in this way. It means only that they could not have been avoided like this in the case of beings very like us. And it invites the question of why God would have created beings like us, when he might, so it seems, have created superior beings.

So, one way in which unintended evils might have been avoided, or largely avoided, would have been if we had had more extensive knowledge. But there is also another way. Things could, surely, have been arranged so that evil could not occur without evil intent. How might this have been achieved? The major problem is that we are creatures with bodies, creatures whose welfare can be affected by states of our bodies. And that makes it rather hard to see how it might be possible for deliberate harm to be done by acting on our bodies, without its also being possible that accidental harm should occur in the same way. Again, one way of achieving this situation would be if God constantly intervened to stop accidental harm. Perhaps this would result in a loss, namely, that the world would be a less intelligible place. Or, if it did not have this result, perhaps it would have the consequence that, to the extent that we could understand why bodies were affected in a damaging way on some occasions but not others, we would be in a position to predict when God would intervene and when he would not. And this might be thought to be an undesirable consequence. However, the same effect could presumably be achieved without either of these consequences, if the *laws of nature* were such that damaging effects could not be produced without evil intent; not because there was some very elaborate arrangement which had this as an indirect consequence—that, even if it were possible, would be liable to make the world unintelligible. The position might rather be that the laws of nature directly concerned evil intent. It would, of course, be a very odd setup. The laws of nature would be very strange, to be sure; but that is not the main point. The real oddity would be the role of our bodies. As things are, our welfare is intimately bound up with the state of our bodies, and our bodies interact with other physical objects in much the same way as physical objects interact with each other. On the set up being envisaged things would be very different. Either our welfare would be affected by states of our bodies—affected for the worse at any rate—only to the extent that the states of our bodies had been brought about by evil intent; or else the ways in which our bodies were affected by other physical objects would depend on the presence or absence of evil intent. Either way our relationship with the physical world, or with the rest of it, would be very different. Again this is not to say that unintended evils are *not* avoidable in this way. Rather, again, it raises the question of why God should have created beings like us. Why should he not have created a world with superior beings, who were not constantly at risk as a result of the inconvenience of being so intimately attached to bodies? So, there is, at any rate, a problem about evils which are the unintended consequences of free choices.

There is also a problem about evils that are not (apparently) the outcome of free choices at all. The most obvious example is suffering by animals. Some animal suffering *is*, of course, the outcome of free choices by humans; but some is not—in particular animal suffering which preceded man. Of course, one could always claim that animals do not in fact suffer; they just behave as if they did. And one might fall back on this answer if one thought that animal suffering would be incompatible with the existence of a perfectly good, omniscient, omnipotent God. But this view would surely not be rational. We surely have better reasons to believe that animals suffer than we have to believe that there exists such a God, whose existence is incompatible with that suffering. It would, of course, also be a very *dangerous* view to hold; dangerous to animals, that is. But that is another matter. Again one could concede that animals suffer, but say that it did not *matter*, that there was nothing *bad* about it. I shall not try to answer that, beyond saying that it seems to have even less to recommend itself than the view that animals do not suffer. What is rather more plausible is the view that animal suffering does not matter as *much* as human suffering. But, even if something like that is true, it does not explain why there should be any, unless it were essential to the avoidance of human suffering.

There is, I think, an answer to the problem of suffering in animals which is related to an answer to the question of why God should have created creatures like us, when he might have created superior beings. But first we should look at two more accounts of why evil might be present in a good world. In fact these accounts suggest a relation between good and evil which is rather different from that suggested by the free will account. On that account the existence of a good depends on the world being such that evil is *possible*. It does not depend on there actually being any evil. Actual evil does not help. God's purposes would not have been frustrated if there had been no evil at all. But, on the accounts I shall consider next, it is the actual existence of evil which contributes to good; the good would not have been possible without the evil.

### Evil and the Good of Knowledge

One sort of good that can come out of evil—out of suffering, for instance—is due to the fact that the observation of how evil can occur can enable us to acquire knowledge by ordinary rational means.[12] But why might that knowledge be good? And would its goodness be enough to make it good that there should actually be evil? Perhaps all knowledge is good in itself; but that will not help. No one would think that the existence of an evil could be made *worthwhile* by the mere fact that it made knowledge of it possible. More to the point, the knowledge might be good, because it would help us to know how to avoid producing evil ourselves, or how to prevent it. Now, it is true that, if we appeal to the free will defence, we can claim that it *is* good that evil should be possible. But the goodness of knowing how to prevent it would not make it good that evil should be *actual*. It could at

---

[12] See Swinburne, *The Existence of God*, 202–14, and *Providence and the Problem of Evil*, ch. 10.

most do *something* (but surely only something) to compensate for it. At least if unintended evil occurs we can *learn* from it. At least if *intended* evil occurs, we can learn from it. But better, from that point of view, to have neither the evil, nor the learning. But there is another way in which the knowledge might contribute to something good. In general the bare freedom to do something is not very valuable; it becomes valuable when we acquire the knowledge of how to exercise the freedom. But that means that having the freedom to do evil together with the knowledge of how to, is more valuable than the bare freedom. It is, of course, also very dangerous. But the free will account emphasizes the value of dangerous freedom. So knowledge of how evil is caused is valuable in this way—not because it means that we know how to *prevent* evil, but because it means that we know how to *produce* it. So evil itself can be valuable in this way—it makes valuable knowledge possible.

So far one might think that this view only pointed to some good that could come out of evil. But actually it could be used to make a stronger claim. It could be argued that it was actually a good thing, all things considered, that there should be some evil in order that there should be rational beliefs about how to produce it. And further, it could be argued that it was a good thing, all things considered, that there should be some *unintended* evils. For if, so to speak, the earliest intended evils were to have been based on rational beliefs about how to produce evil, these beliefs could have arisen only from observing unintended evils.

However, it may be doubted whether such considerations can show that very *much* actual evil is a good thing, all things considered. After all, to take an example, I can form a fairly good idea how to cause enormous pain to others by the use of heat, just on the basis of my limited acquaintance with minor burns, and my observation of the effects of heat on inanimate objects. And it may be further doubted whether it is plausible that any *unintended* evils were necessary. It may be that, but for unintended evils, at least some intended evils must have been based on beliefs which arose by other than ordinary rational means. But even if such beliefs will have been irrational, and even if it is a bad thing that there should be irrational beliefs, it is not clear that it is *worse* than unintended suffering.

So I doubt whether the goodness of rationality can be invoked to explain the actual existence of much, if any, evil. That is not to say that it is not a good thing that we should find the world intelligible. It is surely a very good thing. And it seems rather likely that, if the world is to be intelligible to creatures like us, with our ways of acquiring knowledge, our degree of intelligence, and our physical nature, it is inevitable that there will be unintended evils. This we have, in effect, already seen. But these evils are inevitable in the sense that there is no way of ensuring that they will not occur, without the sacrifice of a good. It is not that they are *required*.

## Soul-making

There is another way in which evils can contribute to good. They can contribute by making it possible for us to be better people. We can be compassionate to those who have suffered and we can help them to overcome their suffering; we can show fortitude and retain hope in the face of our own suffering; we can show courage in the face of danger; we can accept suffering for ourselves to enable others to have better lives. None of these things would be possible if there were no evil. (Or at least a belief that there was evil; but I doubt if anyone would think that the world would have been a better place if our attitudes had been the same, but they had all been based on false beliefs.) Perhaps one might go on to say that, not only can evils contribute to goods in this way, but that a life that has encountered evils and the possibility of evils in this way is a *better* life than one where there have been no such evils to face. Another way of putting this idea would be to say that there is a certain sort of perfection which God desires for us which could only be achieved through the facing of evils. We could not have been created with such perfection ready made.[13]

I think that there is much to be said for this approach. But there are also a number of difficulties. The first difficulty is this. Even if

---

[13] For this approach, see John Hick, *Evil and the God of Love*, 2nd edn. (London: Macmillan, 1977), pt. IV.

evils and the possibility of evils make room for goods which could not otherwise be achieved, they may also occur without any compensating good. What is worse, they may also make room for further *evils* that could not otherwise occur. Suffering in others may be met with indifference, or callousness, or even pleasure. We may face dangers with cowardice, rather than courage. We may act selfishly when there are evils to be faced. We may face suffering with weakness and hopelessness. Now, it is true that it might be replied that this is just parallel to the case of free will. The possibility of free will does indeed make possible bad choices as well as good choices; but, nonetheless, it might be said, it is better that there should be free will than that there should not be. Similarly, it might be said, the value of dealing well with evil depends in part on there being a possibility of dealing badly with it. So that there could not be the possibility of the good, without there being the possibility of the corresponding evil. And it is better that there should be the possibility of both, than that there should be the possibility of neither. I think that there is something in this reply; though it is not entirely unproblematical. The difficulty is that not all these ways of dealing with evil seem to be exercises of *freedom*, or even to stem from prior exercises of freedom. So it is not altogether clear why the value of good ways of dealing with evils should depend at all on there being the possibility of there being bad ways. On the other hand we do seem to think that dealing well with evils is meritorious; which might be considered odd enough if nothing like freedom were present. We do not think of moral beauty as on a footing with physical beauty.

However one might still worry a bit about some of the failures to deal well with evils. The problem is that some of the failures are not of the sort that would normally be regarded as blameworthy. The evils may be such that only a saint could withstand them. We may be too young, too inexperienced, too ordinary. The evils may be so terrible as to crush our spirits, to lead to incomprehension and despair. So, why should the possibility of failure in *these* cases be required in order to make room for the good of dealing well with evils? The second difficulty is that, whereas some of the goods that I mentioned come through evils that we ourselves undergo or are threatened by, others come though evils that others undergo, often involuntarily. I shall discuss a particularly severe form of this problem later. The third difficulty is this. Even if we accept that a certain sort of perfection could not be achieved without evil, that a certain sort of goodness of life depends on there being evil, it seems harder to believe that the *best* sort of life, or the *best* sort of perfection necessarily requires evil.

## Must God Create the Best?

It is time to return to the question of why God should have created us, rather than superior beings of some sort. Or, to put it another way, whether inferior beings such as us could have been created by a perfectly good, omnipotent, omniscient God.[14]

Now, in fact, if we think of God according to the abstract conception, the question does not seem very hard to answer. The question is whether something could exist because it is good, when a better thing could have existed instead. And there seems to be no problem. As long as the thing *is* good—or so it seems at first sight—that is all that is needed if it is to be possible that it exists because it is good. There is no requirement that there could not have been something better. And I am not here appealing to the idea that variety is a good thing—that it is actually *better* that there should be less good good things in addition to better good things. I am just appealing to what seems obvious; that, if something *is* good, there is no problem about supposing that it exists *because* it is good.

What is more, there does not seem to be much more of a problem if we return to the question in its traditional form. Not only does there not seem to be a problem in the idea that a *good* God might create a good thing which was not the best possible thing—although he *could* indeed have created a better thing; not only does this not seem to be a problem, but it does not seem that a problem is introduced if we specify that he is *perfectly* good.

[14] I am indebted in this section to Robert M. Adams, 'Must God Create the Best?' in his *The Virtue of Faith* (Oxford: Oxford University Press, 1987); first published in *Philosophical Review* 81 (1972), 317–32.

There does not seem to be a problem. But are things as they seem?

There is indeed a proviso to be made. There might be a world which was good, even very good, which contained a certain amount of evil. Now, what if this evil were *gratuitous* evil? I mean, what if it did not contribute in any way to the goodness of the world, and it could have been avoided without sacrificing any good features of the world and without making it a very different sort of world. This is perfectly compatible with the world's being a good world (all things considered), but surely we cannot say that *that* world could exist because it was good. The reason is that the gratuitous evil could not, of course, exist because *it* was good; but nor could it exist because something *else* was good, since it is gratuitous. It does not contribute to the goodness of anything, nor does it stem from any essential ingredient in any type of thing which is good. So we were a little hasty in thinking that there was no reason in the case of *any* good thing why it should not exist because it is good. Let us say instead that there is no reason why a good thing *which does not contain any gratuitous evil* should not exist because it is good.

There *is*, in fact, a problem with this claim too, which I shall turn to in the next section. But meanwhile it seems that by appealing to the claim we can deal with some of the problems we have encountered earlier; in particular, the problem of unintended human suffering and the problem of animal suffering. In effect we have, perhaps, already dealt with the former. For it seemed that although unintended human suffering is not, in the abstract, inevitable, it could not be avoided without making humans very different from the way they are; and, surely, *so* different that the evil of unintended suffering could not be said to be a gratuitous evil.

What about animal suffering, and in particular animal suffering in which human choice plays no part? Now, I do not think that it can be said that the degree and extent of this suffering is so evil that it would have been better that there should have been no animals such as we know them at all; or rather, perhaps, that the world should not have been such as to permit the evolution of such animals. So, the existence of animals such as they are is, at least, a good thing. But it cannot be said either that their suffering is a *gratuitous* evil. The reason is, of course, that it performs a useful function. Now, it is true, presumably, that there *could* have been creatures for whom this function was performed by some means which did not *distress* the creatures. But such creatures would have been creatures of a very different sort from animals as we know them; and the world which did not allow the evolution of animals as we know them would have been a very different world. A better world? Perhaps. But that is beside the point if animal suffering is not a gratuitous evil.

And here I want to return to human beings. In discussing human suffering I made much of free will and the goodness of it. But what if there is no such thing as free will? Does that mean that this world cannot after all have been created by a good God? Surely not. Surely, even if there is no free will, it is not *bad* that human beings should exist. And surely, even if human suffering, and the suffering caused by humans, is very evil, it is not a *gratuitous* evil, any more than animal suffering and the suffering which animals cause is gratuitous. Even if there is no free will, the suffering that humans undergo and the suffering they cause, result from our being the sorts of creatures we are. And even if we are not as good as creatures might have been, we are surely not, taken as a whole, *bad*.

### Terrible Lives

It seems that this world is good, even if there might have been better worlds. It seems also that it does not contain gratuitous evil. Is this enough to make it plausible that it exists because it is good that it should? Is it enough to make it possible that it was created by a perfectly good, omnipotent, omniscient God? There is one problem, and it is, I think, the biggest problem of all. Could such a God have created a system in which some lives were not worth living? There is no great problem, perhaps, about lives which are not as good as they might have been—not as good for the people themselves, that is. That is no more of a problem than the existence of a world which is not as good as it could have been. But what about really terrible lives; lives of which it could be said that it would have been better for the person if he had never existed? Could a perfectly good God create a world with such lives in it? Could a *loving* God create such a world? But it seems that there *are* such lives.

Let us first consider whether such a world could really be a good world. Or would this fact, that it contained some people whose lives were so awful that it would have been better for them that they had never existed, would this fact mean that it would have been better that the world had never existed? I think that it would not. Here is a consideration which might help. Suppose that someone were in a position where he could do some great good by sacrificing everything, by undergoing terrible suffering culminating in his death. And I do mean sacrificing everything that might make his life good for him. We are not, for instance, to suppose that during his suffering he could have the satisfaction of appreciating the good he was doing. Let us suppose, instead, that at that time the suffering would seem wholly bad, incomprehensible even. And suppose he chose to do this. We would surely think this an admirable thing to have done. Now, of course, what makes it admirable is that he *chose* to do this. But must we not also suppose that, *independently of this fact*, the good to be achieved was worth the suffering? That is what *he* thought. It was no part of his calculation that his moral virtue would tip the balance. And surely we do not want to say that he was *wrong* about this; that what he did was based on a glorious mistake. This does not mean, of course, that if he had *not* made the heroic choice, it would have been all right for someone to compel him. It is quite possible that it would be wrong for us to compel someone to do something which was nonetheless good. That is what liberty is about. But it *does* seem to mean that, if this terrible sacrifice had taken place, uncompelled by us, but also *unchosen*, the good would have been worth the suffering. Is that not what we would think? We might greatly regret that he was not able to appreciate the value of his sacrifice; we might wish that we somehow had it in our power to make him see this, to thank him for what he had done, however unintended. (As we think it right to remember with gratitude those who fought and died in wars, even though their sacrifice may have been quite involuntary.) But none of that need make us think that the good was not worth it.

But even if it could be good that there should be such a world, could a perfectly good God create it? Could a *loving* God create it?

There are two worries here, I think. The first is that we might think that it would be wrong for God to create such a world for the same reason as it would be wrong for us to compel the person to make the sacrifice. But, even on the traditional conception of God, *that* consideration need not detain us. The fact that *we* have no right to compel people to do certain things does not mean that their creator does not.[15] The more important worry is the worry about a loving God. If he cares for me so much, how could he let me suffer so much? But surely we *have* an answer to that question. He lets you suffer so much because there are other good things which would not otherwise be obtainable. He loves you; but you are not the only thing he loves; you are not the only thing he cares about.

It would be as well to be clear about something. In my example, where the person sacrificed his good, the sacrifice was deliberate, was planned. However, on some accounts, especially the free will account, most, if not all, human suffering will not have been planned by God. It will have been inevitable only in the sense that God could not have ensured that it did not happen. And even in the case of animal suffering something similar seems to be the case. If one supposes that the world is not a deterministic world, and that this lack of determinism is not a mere detail, but an essential constituent, then the suffering of animals will also have been inevitable, but not planned. So, why should I consider an example where the evil was actually planned? The answer is simple. It is, surely, harder to explain how a loving God could have planned terrible lives for some people in creating the world, than to explain how he could have created a world in which such lives were inevitable; or, if not harder, at least not easier. So, if that if the former task can be accomplished, so can the latter.

There is a final point. I have mentioned that we might wish that we had it in our power to get a person to appreciate the value of his unintended sacrifice, and to thank him for it. *We* will generally lack such a power, but *God* will not. So it is tempting to think that he will exercise the power, either in this life or in an after life. But it is important, I think, that we do not appeal to such an idea in dealing with the problem of evil, in the absence of any evidence that he does exercise

<hr>

[15] See Swinburne, *Providence and the Problem of Evil*, ch. 12.

such a power. And it is perhaps important that we should *not* have
any evidence that God will make the sufferer's suffering worthwhile
for him after all. To know this would, perhaps, tempt us to think that
what we do does not so very much matter. We cannot in the end do
appalling evil; we cannot in the end make a real sacrifice. So, perhaps,
it is better that we should not know; but, perhaps, it is not wrong to
hope.

And how does this look from point of view of the abstract conception? On that conception we can say that it could indeed be the
case that the world was good in spite of this person's terrible suffering; that although in itself the suffering was very bad, and it would
have been better just from this point of view that there should not
have been any such suffering, nonetheless it was better that these
other goods should have been achieved at its expense, rather than that
neither should have existed. It would also be good that the person's
suffering could be made to seem worthwhile to *him*; that *he* could
think of his life as, after all, worthwhile; so that it *would* be worthwhile even for him; so that it would not be the case that for him it
would have been better if he had never existed. And there is no
impossibility that this should happen, and should happen because it
is good that it should. So we may *hope* that this is so, but that is all.
It is one thing to believe that the world is good, and exists because it
is good. It is another thing to conclude that, because something else
would be good, it must be a reality also.

# 7

## Miracles

IN CHAPTERS 4 AND 5 I argued that it would be reasonable to believe in God conceived in a certain way. The belief discussed was the belief in a creator God; the belief that the world exists because it is good that a world like this should exist. I also argued in chapter 5 that there would be no difficulty in principle in supposing that God, so conceived, could act in the world. That would be the case if something were to happen more or less directly because it was good that it should happen. What I want to consider in this chapter is whether we could in practice have a good reason to suppose that God had in fact acted in the world on a certain occasion.

It is natural, in this connection, to think of miracles. And one could rephrase the question as, 'Could we have a good reason to believe that a miracle had occurred?' The questions, though, are not *quite* equivalent. In the first place, something would not count as a miracle, perhaps, unless it were in some way *surprising*. So miracles could not be *commonplace*. I shall not be interested in that feature of miracles. Secondly, although a miracle might stem immediately from divine action, the role of divine action might be more indirect. So that the apostles, for instance, may be thought of as performing miracles, the divine action consisting in this case in the conferring of abnormal powers. But, with those caveats, we may think of our question as a question about miracles.

### Miracles as 'Violations of the Laws of Nature'

Let me first clear up a possible confusion about the relation between miracles and the laws of nature. The source of the confusion lies in the fact that it is natural to think of miracles as in some sense *violations* of laws of nature.[1] But, if one thinks this, things can seem rather puzzling. Indeed it might seem that one could tell at the outset that there could not possibly *be* any such thing as a miracle. For how, one might wonder, could there possibly be such a thing as a violation of a law of nature. It is not as if laws of nature are like laws of the land, which say how subjects *should* behave. The laws of nature are in no danger of being disobeyed by recalcitrant atoms. If something is a law of nature, must it not be at least a *true* statement, not about what *should* happen in nature, but about what actually *does* happen in nature? But, in that case, how could there be a violation?

The answer is that there indeed could not be any such thing as a violation of a law of nature; but, for events to qualify as miracles they do not have involve anything that could properly be called a violation of a law of nature. They may, however, involve something enough like it to explain why this description might seem apt.

Miracles are cases of God's acting in the world, as opposed to cases where things happen as they do because of the way he created the world. So, they are indeed cases where things do not happen as they do *because* the laws of nature are as they are. They happen just because it is good that they should happen so, rather than because of what the laws of nature say. But to say that things do not happen because of the laws of nature is not, of course, to say that they happen *in violation of* the laws of nature. Indeed it is not so far even *tempting* to describe things like that. So, why might one be tempted to think of a miracle as a violation of the laws of nature? To answer that question we need to notice that there are two different ways in which a miraculous happening may be related to the laws of nature. The first way is when what happens is something that *could* have happened in those circumstances in the ordinary course of nature—though presumably on this occasion it is not true that it *would* have

---

[1] 'A miracle may be accurately defined, *a transgression of a law of nature by a particular volition of the Deity, or by the interposition of some invisible agent*': Hume, *An Enquiry Concerning Human Understanding*, 115 n.

happened without God's intervention: why, otherwise would he have intervened? This could be the case if the laws governing how things behave are probabilistic, rather than deterministic. Consider a trivial example. Let us suppose that how a die lands is not determined by the way it is constructed, the way it is thrown, and so on. Suppose that I throw the die on a certain occasion, and I get a six because God makes the die land like that. Now there was nothing in the laws of nature to determine that I would *not* get a six. It would have been perfectly consistent with them that I should have got a six, without any intervention by God. Nonetheless, getting a six *was* a miracle. The die's landing the way it did was a consequence of God's acting; it was not simply the outcome of nature's taking its course. Here, then, we have an example of a miracle where it does not seem at all apt to describe what happens as a violation of the laws of nature. It would not even be very apt if God made me get twelve sixes in a row (or a hundred). This *could* happen in nature; though it would, of course, be very unlikely.

But God's intervention could be rather different. He could intervene in such a way that what happens *could not* have happened in those circumstances if nature had been left to its own devices. Let us suppose that it is a law of nature that no body can move faster than the speed of light. We would have an example of the second sort of intervention if God were to move a die from New York to London in one thousandth of a second. The law of nature does *not*, of course, say that *this* could not happen. It says nothing about what God might or might not do. All the laws of nature are concerned with is what happens when nothing interferes with the workings of nature.[2] So, even in this case, it would not be strictly correct to call such a thing a *violation* of the law. But it is, at least, a little tempting to do so; and it is, I take it, the sort of thing that people have in mind when they think of miracles as being violations. Indeed I shall find it convenient in what follows to describe such an event as inconsistent with the laws of nature—meaning just that it would be inconsistent with the laws of nature that such an event should occur without intervention from outside nature.

---

[2] See Mackie, *The Miracle of Theism*, ch. 1.

## Could We Have a Good Reason for Believing that a
## Miracle Had Occurred?

There are a number of things that might be in doubt in connection
with the question of whether a supposed miraculous event had taken
place. First, it might be in doubt whether the supposed event had
occurred at all. Did water become wine? Was a blind man made to
see? Did Mary win the lottery? Secondly, it might be in doubt
whether the event was actually inconsistent with what were *believed*
to be the laws of nature. Thirdly, it might be in doubt whether the
event was inconsistent with the *actual* laws of nature. And fourthly,
it might be in doubt whether it was God who was involved, rather
than some other supernatural agent.

The first two doubts are not, of course, independent. Normally, to
the extent that we think that something really is inconsistent with
what we believe to be the laws of nature, we will think that it cannot
have happened. Perhaps it was an illusion—the magician could not
*really* have sawn the lady in half without killing her, because such
things are (we suppose) not physically possible. Or perhaps the person who reported it was mistaken or lying. And so on. But this problem should not be exaggerated. It clearly *is* possible to have a good
reason to think that something has occurred which is inconsistent
with what one had till then believed to be the laws of nature; for otherwise we should never have a good reason to revise our views about
the laws of nature. One ought to note, however, that it is likely to be
somewhat easier to be confident that an anomalous event has
occurred in cases where one is inclined to think that the laws of
nature need revising, than in cases where one is inclined to think that
a miracle was involved. One important reason is this. In the case of
the revision of laws it may well be that one can reproduce the circumstances in which the anomalous event was supposed to have
occurred, and in so doing (apparently) reproduce the anomalous
event. Better still, others can reproduce the circumstances, and can
reproduce the event. This matters because, where laws of nature are
involved, it is to be expected that the same event will occur in the same
circumstances—at least this is true where the laws are deterministic

laws. And so, to the extent that the event can apparently be reproduced by repeating the experiment, one can be more confident that
the original event really did occur. But no such source of confidence
is likely to be available in the case of an event which one was inclined
to think was miraculous. This is because it is *not* to be expected that
God will always act in the same way in the same circumstances.
Indeed, to the extent that the event *was* reproducible, one might be
inclined to think that the event had a natural explanation.

Similar considerations suggest that one will be in a stronger position to defend the hypothesis that the laws ought to be revised in
such-and-such a way, than to defend the belief that this event was
miraculous. In the case of the defence of the revision of the laws,
more experiments can be performed, and (if they yield the predicted
results) can help to confirm the hypothesis. But, in the absence of
laws determining his behaviour, this is not going to be possible in the
case of the hypothesis that God brought this about. And this advantage, which the defender of the revision of the laws has over the
defender of the view that a miracle has occurred, does not require
that the laws in question should be deterministic. It would obtain
equally in the case of probabilistic laws. It is true that such a law will
not imply that a certain event will always occur in certain circumstances; so it will not be straightforwardly confirmed or disconfirmed
by the occurrence or non-occurrence of the event. It will, though,
assign a certain probability to the occurrence of the event in given
circumstances. And, although no actual frequency of occurrences
would show that one was *certainly* wrong about the law, to the extent
that the actual frequency diverges from what might be expected given
the probability, it will be more or less unlikely that the law is correct.
Consider, by way of analogy, the hypothesis that a coin is unbiased.
Although it is indeed *possible* for an unbiased coin to turn up heads
a hundred times in succession, it is very unlikely that a coin which
turns up heads a hundred times in succession is in fact unbiased. But
equally, if a coin comes up heads about fifty times in a hundred tosses
it is unlikely that it is heavily biased; because it is unlikely for a heavily biased coin to come up heads about half the time in so many
tosses. So, in the case of the hypothesis that a certain probabilistic law
obtains, to the extent that the frequency of the occurrence of the

event is what would be likely if the hypothesis were correct, and unlikely if the hypothesis were wrong, the frequency supports the hypothesis. But no considerations of this sort are likely to be available to someone who wants to defend the hypothesis that a miracle has occurred. He is no more likely to suppose that God's actions are governed by probabilistic laws than that they are governed by deterministic laws. So the frequency with which the supposed miraculous event occurs in the relevant circumstances will not support the hypothesis that a miracle has occurred in the way in which the frequency of an event will support the hypothesis that the event is governed by a probabilistic law.

So far I have suggested that it is likely to be somewhat harder to be reasonably sure that the anomalous event has occurred in cases where one is inclined to think that the event is miraculous, compared with cases where one is inclined to think that the laws may need revising; and somewhat harder to defend the view that the event was miraculous than to defend the view that the laws should be revised in a certain way. But there is a further problem for someone who wants to defend the claim that an event was miraculous. The problem is that, even if he has a good reason to suppose that an event has occurred which is inconsistent with currently accepted laws, he will need in addition a good reason to believe that the event is miraculous, rather than that it has an explanation in natural terms. And there is a particular difficulty about this. To bring out this difficulty, let us suppose that the situation is as favourable as possible for the hypothesis that the event was a miracle. Let us suppose that there are very good reasons for supposing that it was inconsistent with the currently accepted laws, and that the event was good. The latter will, of course, be necessary if we are to have a reason to think that *God* caused the event, rather than some other supernatural agent. Now one possible hypothesis is indeed that the event was miraculous; that is, that it happened just because it was good that it should happen. Will there be any competing hypotheses which do not invoke God? Well, there may be a number, but the crucial fact is that there is bound to be at least *one* such hypothesis, which is at least as well supported by the facts, or so it seems. Remember that if the event was indeed a good event in those circumstances, there must be facts of the matter in virtue of

which it was good that such an event should occur in these circumstances. Now the alternative hypothesis will be that the event
occurred, not because it was good that such an event should occur in
circumstances like that (not because God caused it), but just because
the circumstances were like that. That is to say, the *goodness* played
no part. Of course, the natural explanation might be very different
from the sorts of natural explanation we are used to. But then an
explanation which appealed to the fact that it was good that such an
event should occur would be very different, in so far as the goodness
operated directly, rather than through the perceptions of natural
intelligent beings like us. So, could there be a good reason for preferring the explanation which appeals to goodness, to God, compared
with the competing explanation which does not?

Perhaps there *could* be a good reason for thinking that goodness
played a part. Perhaps our evidence is not restricted to what has happened on just one occasion. Perhaps there have been a number of
events, all of which appear to have no ordinary sort of natural explanation, and all of which are events which are good in the circumstances. Might it not be the case that, although they *could* be
explained by appeal simply to the natural features of the case, in
virtue of which the events were indeed good, there would be a *better*
explanation in terms of the fact that the events were good? For, the
natural features, in virtue of which the various events were good,
might not fit into any pattern, when looked at simply as natural features. What made *this* event good in *these* circumstances might be
very different from what made *that* good in *those* circumstances. But
once one took into account the *goodness* of the events a pattern might
emerge. Might it not in that case be reasonable to think that the
explanation for the events was indeed that it was good that such-and-
such should occur? Perhaps it might. But even if it did, that would
not mean that it was reasonable to believe that here was a miracle.
The reason is that goodness might feature in the explanation in a different way. Instead of explaining the particular event directly, it
might instead explain why there was a natural law relating to the
occurrence of this sort of event in circumstances of this sort. So the
explanation was not that these events occurred in these circumstances
simply because it was good that they should; but that they occurred

in these circumstances because there was a law that they should (or should sometimes); and the law was as it was because it was good that there should be such a law. And, if that were the correct account, the events would not after all be miraculous. So it seems that, even if one were in the best possible position to believe that a miracle had occurred, there would always be an alternative hypothesis which was at least as well supported by the facts, the hypothesis according to which goodness did in fact play *some* part, but not a direct part. Are things as they seem?

## Why Should God React to the World?

The position is this. We have, at best, two competing accounts. According to one, God reacts to things which occur in the world; he causes good things to happen in the light of these occurrences. According to the other, everything is arranged as part of the creation. The question is whether there is any reason to prefer the first account to the second.

It seems that, as long as we simply consider what evidence might be available in terms of events in the world, the answer is going to be 'No'. Indeed, if either account is going to be preferred, it seems likely that it will be the account according to which everything is settled as part of the creation, since it seems *simplest* to suppose that the role of goodness with respect to the natural order is confined to the creation. If we are going to have a reason to prefer the account according to which God reacts, it will have to be, I think, because there is something good that he could achieve if he reacted to things in the world, which he could not achieve by making suitable provision as part of the creation. How might this be?

One possibility that might occur to one is that it is necessary for God to react to what happens in the world in order that what occurs should be *appropriate*, should fit the circumstances. For, one might think, the appropriateness or otherwise of an event might depend on facts that were not available to God at the creation. The reason for thinking this might be that its appropriateness might depend on people's free choices, and that these could not be known at the creation—for reasons that I have discussed in Chapter 6. But this reason for preferring the account in terms of reaction would be a poor one. To know what would be appropriate in what circumstances, it is not necessary for God to know what circumstances are actually going to arise. So, there is no reason why he should not ensure the appropriateness of what happens by providing for it as part of the creation, by providing for it in the nature of the laws.

Another suggestion might go as follows. If the good effects were the result of the operation of laws, it would be possible for us to predict when they would occur; whereas if they were the result of God's reacting, it would not be possible—at least on the assumption that God's actions were not dictated by laws. And it might be thought that this inability on our part to predict might be a good thing. What would be good about it? Perhaps it would be good because it would mean that we would be unable to manipulate things in such a way as to produce results we desired, and it might be thought that it was good for us not to be able to manipulate things—perhaps because such an ability would give rise to an undesirable attitude. Maybe there is something in this, although it could hardly be claimed that this inability to predict was *always* a good thing; that it was *always* a bad thing to be able to manipulate things, or (to describe things less tendentiously) to produce results in predictable ways. But we need not pursue this question. It will be enough to notice that, even if the inability to predict would be a good thing in the relevant cases, it could be achieved just as well by the existence of laws of a suitable sort. One way it might be achieved would be if the laws in question were probabilistic, and the occurrence of 'miraculous' events were relatively rare. Then, not only would it be impossible to predict the occurrence of the event with any certainty, it would also be impossible even to assign a probability to the occurrence of the event with any confidence. So, we would no more be able to manipulate things by exploiting the laws than we would be able to manipulate God.

The previous suggestion was that it would be better if God were to produce good effects by reacting rather than by providing for them at the creation, since the latter arrangement would be more likely to give rise to an undesirable attitude on our part. A somewhat similar suggestion might go like this. Consider a case where an action of ours gives rise to the good event. To the extent that we thought that this was the result simply of the operation of laws, we might think of the event as having been brought about by us, as being *our* work. But, if we thought of the event as arising from God's reaction to our action, as arising from his free choice, we would not think of ourselves as being responsible. And, the suggestion continues, the latter attitude is better, the attitude that *we* are not responsible, that the event occurred by the grace of God, let us say. But I do not think that this suggestion is very persuasive. Perhaps some people *might* be somewhat less likely to have an undesirable attitude if they thought of the event as due to God's reaction, but there would be nothing *rational* about giving oneself more credit, so to speak, in the case where the event was the result of the operation of laws. In both cases what one did played *some* part—the good event occurred because of what one did. But in neither case was it all one's own work. In the one case the event will, of course, have depended on God's reacting in a certain way; but in the other case it will have depended on God's having made laws of a certain sort.

So are there any better suggestions as to why it might be better if God reacted (in some cases) than if he arranged the laws in suitable ways? I think the suggestion that has the best chance of succeeding is that there is something good *in itself* about God's reacting. It is not that some extraneous good can be achieved in that way; rather, there is something intrinsically good about reaction—appropriate reaction, of course. Could this be made plausible? I think that it could by appeal to a natural thought—though, it must be said, a rather elusive thought. The thought is that people matter as *individuals*, not just as being people of a certain sort. This thought is reflected in the idea that I mentioned in Chapter 5, the idea that God cares about *me*. It is not just that he wills the good of any person, or of any person of such-and-such a sort. He wills *my* good. He loves *me*. But to think this is to think there is something *good* about God's caring about me, loving me. And since the most straightforward manifestation of God's love would involve his *reacting* to me and my situation in some way, this seems to mean that it is *good* that he should react to my situation. And notice that, on this thought, the good of God's caring about me, loving me, is not some *extraneous* good which could be achieved thereby — any extraneous good could be achieved just as well by providing for any person like me; it need not be provided with *me* in mind. So there does seem to be something intuitively attractive in the idea that it would be better, *intrinsically* better, if God reacted in some cases, better that sometimes things should happen just because it was good that they should.

Nonetheless, we should be cautious about supposing that this provides a good reason for supposing that miracles occur. In the first place it is not so obvious that it *would* be a good thing for God to intervene in the workings of the world. There are some reasons to suppose otherwise. For instance, considerations about the goodness of human freedom, which I discussed in Chapter 6, suggest that it would be better that he should *not* intervene. But, in any case, even if it would be good that miracles should occur, that some events should occur just because it was good that they should, that would at most render it unsurprising if such things should happen. It would not provide us with a reason for supposing that they actually do. We have, of course, no reason to believe that everything which would be good actually is the case.

## Uninferred Beliefs in Miracles

There is one final possibility which I ought to mention. In asking whether we could have a good reason for believing that God had acted in the world, I have been writing as if to have a good reason for this would be a matter of being in a good position to *infer* that it was so on the basis of evidence—in particular, on the basis of reasonable beliefs about the world which were not themselves beliefs about God. But perhaps one could have a reasonable belief that God had acted in the world without that belief having been inferred from other beliefs.[3] To see how this might be so, consider the following outline of

---

[3] For the idea that we may have reasonable uninferred beliefs about God see, for instance, Alvin Plantinga, 'Reason and Belief in God', Alston, William P., 'Christian

an account of reasonableness. According to this account, an uninferred belief has, when considered in isolation, a minimal degree of
reasonableness. Whether it has more than a minimal degree of reasonableness, or whether, on the contrary, it is actually unreasonable,
depends on its relations with other beliefs which the believer has. To
the extent that the belief in question forms part of a coherent set
beliefs, it is reasonable; to the extent that it contributes to incoher-
ence in the set of beliefs, it will be unreasonable, if coherence could
best be increased by abandoning it. Now, the details of the account
are not important. Clearly, anything more than a sketch would have
to spell out what coherence consists in; and it does not terribly matter whether the account confers a minimal degree of reasonableness
on an uninferred belief, other things being equal, or whether it
regards such a belief as neutral as far as reasonableness goes. The crucial feature of the account is that it is the relation between a person's
beliefs which determines their reasonableness.[4] That being so,
whether a particular belief is reasonable or not will depend critically
on what other beliefs the person has. So, it must surely be *possible* for
a person to have a reasonable uninferred belief that God has acted in
the world, especially if he has a large number of mutually corrobor-
ating beliefs of this sort. It could hardly be that *no* set of beliefs, of
which this was a member, could have the required degree of coherence. And, actually, one might go a little further. One might add that,
if it is possible for someone to have a reasonable uninferred belief
that God has acted in the world, it will also be possible for someone
to believe this reasonably on the basis of inference. For, one might
suggest, just as an uninferred belief has, other things being equal, a
minimal degree of reasonableness, so too it is minimally reasonable,
on the basis of the fact that someone else has an uninferred belief, to
infer that what he believes is the case. Though, of course, whether
such a inference will be *actually* reasonable or not will again depend

---

Experience and Christian Belief', and Nicholas Wolterstoff, 'Can Belief in God be
Rational if it Has No Foundations?', all in Alvin Plantinga and Nicholas Wolterstoff
(eds.), *Faith and Rationality* (Notre Dame, Ind.: University of Notre Dame Press,
1986); also William P. Alston, *Perceiving God* (Ithaca, N.Y.: Cornell University Press,
1991).

    [4] For a detailed account see BonJour, *The Structure of Empirical Knowledge.*

on the other beliefs of the person making the inference. And, in my case, my beliefs are such that I would be rather unlikely to put much weight on someone else's uninferred belief that God had brought something about directly. I would be unlikely to believe that the way this person's belief had been formed was sufficiently reliably connected to the truth of the matter, to enable me to conclude that here was something which had been brought about directly by God, rather than indirectly by way of natural causes. But others, of course, may be differently placed.

### God's Role in the World

Let me add one thing. One might think that if miracles did not occur, that would mean that God's role in the world was confined to the creation. He wound it up, so to speak, and then abandoned it. This would be quite wrong. It would be to overlook the fact that God's will, on the account I am offering, plays a constant and extensive part in what happens in the world. It plays this part through our perception of what is good. This role does not, of course, consist in the performance of miracles. And it would be misleading to think of it as God's acting in the world. But it is a role, nonetheless, by which God affects what happens, not by *making* good things happen, but by providing *us* with the opportunity of making them happen, of doing his will. He guides, but does not constrain. In fact one of the virtues that might be claimed for the abstract conception of God is precisely that, on this account, it is possible for us to have a constant direct relationship with God, without there being any need for the constant occurrence of miracles.

# The Importance of Rational Belief

I HAVE BEEN ARGUING that it is reasonable to believe in God, when conceived of in a certain way. In this chapter I want to consider whether it *matters* that belief in God should be reasonable; whether, indeed, it is even desirable that it should be. I shall then go on to consider a rather different question—whether it is important that one should believe in God at all.

### Is it Important that Belief in God Should Be Reasonable?

Reasonableness is no doubt a virtue that beliefs can have; but it is not the only virtue. Truth is also a virtue. Someone might indeed claim that truth was the primary virtue of beliefs, and reasonableness was a virtue only because it was conducive to truth. I think that the latter claim is too strong. If it were right, it would be better that we should be programmed with true beliefs, at least on important issues, rather than that we should work things out for ourselves. But this is surely not so. But whether it is right or not, we cannot, of course, conclude that we should stop worrying about whether our beliefs are reasonable or not, and worry instead about whether they are true or not. Perhaps we should not worry about either. But in so far as we are interested in having true beliefs, what are we to do other than do our best to think reasonably? Is there any other way of making it likely that we shall arrive at true beliefs?

Actually one might think that there *could* be no other way. For consider any way we might have of arriving at beliefs. Surely, if we thought that that way of arriving at beliefs made it likely that our beliefs would be true, it was *bound* to be a reasonable way. In fact, however, this does not follow. There is an alternative. But I shall argue that it is not a very attractive alternative for a reasonably intelligent person; at any rate, when what is in question is a belief in God.

### Deference to Authority

In the ordinary course of events we believe what other people tell us, other things being equal. And this is, of course, an entirely reasonable way of arriving at beliefs. But our habit of belief is a habit of believing only *other things being equal*. If we have reasons to think that the person is not telling the truth, it may not be reasonable to believe him; if we have reasons to believe that things are other than he says, it may not be reasonable to believe him. Contrast this ordinary habit of belief with something rather different—deference to authority, as we might call it. Suppose that we *always* believed a certain person on a certain topic; we always ignored any contrary evidence there might be—evidence that on this occasion he might be interested in deceiving us, evidence that things were not as he said. Suppose that we ignored such contrary evidence however good it seemed to be. In that case, surely, our beliefs would not be reasonable. But in spite of that we could have a good reason for thinking that to believe this person unquestioningly on this topic was likely to generate true beliefs, and more likely to generate true beliefs than if we allowed ourselves to think about the question. Suppose, for instance, that we knew ourselves to be very bad at doing arithmetical calculations, and concluded that *however* careful we were, and *however* absurd our authority's answer seemed to be, it was always more likely that he was right. That might make it important to ignore the evidence in any particular case. For, if we allowed ourselves to think about the question, it might well seem to us that on *this* occasion he just could not be right, even taking into account all the occasions in the past when we had been wrong and he had been right. Best not to allow ourselves to think at all. Now, this would seem to be a case where we had a good reason to think that an *irrational* way of arriving at beliefs was more likely generate true beliefs than a rational way.

Could this possibly apply in the case of beliefs about God? Could it possibly be that in so far as we wanted to maximize our chances of having true beliefs on this topic, it was best to defer to authority? Could it be that it was better for us to be irrational in this way, and that we had a good reason to think that it was better? Well, it is perhaps not *absolutely* impossible, but it is difficult to see how it could actually happen in the case of the belief that God exists, at least in the case of any reasonably intelligent person. The difficulty is that, to defer to you (in the face of all evidence) I am going to need to have a pretty good reason to suppose that you are more likely to be right on this sort of topic. But what *sort* of topic are we thinking of? To what sort of area does the question of the existence of God belong? Perhaps, if I were a child, the area would simply be questions that are at all difficult to answer; and it might well be reasonable for me to defer to my parents on the grounds that they were more likely to be right on such questions than me. Their track record, in so far as I was able to judge, would, no doubt, be better than mine on almost everything. But I am not a child. So what am I to judge the area to be? Perhaps it is the area of metaphysical questions. But there are problems about this. I might indeed have a good reason to think that you are much more likely to be right than me over questions of what is necessarily true and what is possibly true. There is some scope for me to have been in a position to compare our track records on these questions: I have frequently found my beliefs to be inconsistent, whereas yours have not been; when I have thought more about issues, I have often come to see that you must be right, whereas you have not come to see that I must be right. So, I might have a reason to defer to you on the question of whether it was metaphysically possible for God to exist, or metaphysically necessary that he should exist. But suppose that that is not at issue. Suppose that it is accepted that it is possible for God to exist, and the question is whether he actually *does* exist. It is not at all clear that I could have a good reason to treat you as an authority on *that*.

But even if the answer is that I *could* have a good reason to treat you as an authority on the question of whether God exists, this would not be especially interesting. It would merely show that some human beings could have a good reason to think that they were less well equipped than others to form rational views on the question. It would be much more interesting if *all* human beings were ill equipped in this way compared with an alternative source. But I have *no* reason to believe in any such alternative source; I have no reason to believe that there is a source which I ought to believe uncritically, if I am to maximize my chances of being right on the question of whether God exists. And actually, if I am to do what I have reason to think will maximize my chances of being right on this issue, I shall not defer to a human authority either. I shall use my powers of reason to the best of my ability.

### The Virtue of Trust

We ought, however, to consider two other reasons which might be advanced for thinking that, on the question of the existence of God, rationality is not important. More specifically they are reasons for thinking that, in certain cases, it can be a good thing to have beliefs, even when the evidence suggests that the beliefs are unlikely to be true.

The first idea emphasizes the virtue of *trust*. For example, when I was a child, it was right for me to trust my parents, even when it seemed that what they were doing was not in my interest. Or, to take another example, perhaps it is sometimes right for a husband to trust his wife, even when the evidence points to her infidelity. Or, it was right for Abraham to trust God to the extent to being of being prepared to sacrifice Isaac. So, sometimes it is right to have beliefs even when the evidence is against them. Should examples such as these persuade us that belief in God is right, even if the evidence is against it? Surely not. For what it is worth, it is quite unclear that these examples are in fact cases where it is good to have an irrational belief. It is just as plausible to interpret them, not as cases where it is good to have blind faith, but rather as cases where there is plenty of *past* evidence in favour of the trustworthiness of the person, and where what is wrong is to give too much weight to the present contrary evidence. But in any case the belief in God is quite different from these examples. *They* are cases where someone already has reasons to believe in the *existence* of someone; the question being whether they should trust the person. It would hardly be reasonable to hold that I owe it to my parents to believe that they *exist*, and that I betray a lack of trust if I do not; or that I owe it to them to believe that they are doing their best for me, if I have no reason even to believe that they exist. Similarly it is difficult to see how I could owe it to God to believe that he exists. But even if *this* were true, even if I did owe it to God to believe that he exists, I certainly have no *reason* to think that I owe him this, unless I have a reason to think that he exists.


### Pascal's Wager


The second idea is the idea behind Pascal's wager.[1] The idea is that, if God exists, it is very important indeed that I should believe that he does—Pascal's idea was that salvation (that is to say, eternal bliss) depended on it. If, on the other hand he does not exist, nothing much is lost if I believe falsely that he exists. So even if it is very unlikely indeed that he exists, it is, so to speak, a good *bet* to believe that he exists. Just as it would be a good bet to pay a pound for a lottery ticket, even if the chances of winning were only one in a million, if the prize were ten million pounds. (Or would be, if one made some obvious, if false, assumptions about the value of winning ten million pounds.) Such a belief in God might be an irrational belief, in the sense that the evidence was heavily in favour of its falsehood. But it would be rational to have the belief in the sense that it would be *prudent* to have it.


[1] Blaise Pascal, *Pensées*, trans. Honor Levi (Oxford: Oxford University Press, 1999), 152–6.

The argument does not, however, succeed. There is, to start with, a problem about the probability to be assigned to the proposition that, if I have an irrational belief in God, I will achieve salvation, *if* God exists. One might rather think that, if God does exist, he will *not* value irrational belief; and I will gain nothing from having such a belief. Of course the defender of the wager need not be defeated immediately by this move. He can say that, even if the probability is relatively low that, if God exists, irrational belief will be rewarded by eternal bliss, nonetheless the value of eternal bliss is so great as to make the bet still a good bet. But now we should notice that not all the relevant calculations of expected payouts have been performed. We need to take into account the possibility that God might punish with eternal damnation those who have been content to have irrational beliefs in him on the basis of this sort of consideration. Perhaps the probability of *this* is also very small. But this must be set against the enormity of the cost. Again we would have to take into account the possibility that God does not exist at all, or at least not a God who is in any sense benevolent, but that there exists instead a being of enormous malice who would punish believers in God with eternal pain. Once all these calculations have been performed it is not clear that we have a good bet at all.

There is, in any case, a quite general problem of how to assign probabilities to such propositions as that there is a God who will reward irrational belief in him with eternal bliss; or that there is a demon who will mete out eternal pain to believers in God. These are alike propositions which, for all that has been said, we have no *positive* reason to believe at all. The only thing to be said for them is that they are both apparently logically possible. And one should not be tempted to say that in that case their probabilities are equal. If we assign equal probabilities to propositions about which we are equally ignorant we will soon land ourselves in contradictions. Consider the following example. Suppose I am a visitor from outer space and, having come across a standard six-faced die for the first time, try to assess the probability of a six coming up. If I adopt the principle of assigning equal probabilities to propositions about which I am equally ignorant, I will say that there is one chance in six of a six coming up, because there are six possible outcomes (one, two, three, four, five, and six), and I know nothing else about their likelihoods. But I will *also* say that there is one chance in *two* of a six, because are *two* possible outcomes (six and something other than six). Indeed *no* assessment of the chances would be ruled out. The moral is that the calculations which Pascal's wager requires just cannot be performed.

Let me consider one objection to what I have just said. Suppose, the objection goes, that someone, say John, did as a matter of fact assign a higher probability to the existence of a God who would reward believers with eternal bliss than to the existence of a malicious being who would reward believers with eternal torment. Then surely it would be rational for John (if we make suitable assumptions about his other beliefs) to believe in God; just as it would be rational for me to bet a pound on a horse, if I thought that I would win three pounds if it won, and that the chances of its doing so were even.[2] However, for all that has been said, this bet would be merely *subjectively* rational. It would be rational merely *relative to my beliefs*. And, if these beliefs themselves were quite irrational, the bet would be *objectively* irrational. So it is with John's bet on the existence of God. Perhaps the bet would be subjectively rational; but it would not be objectively rational unless his assignment of probabilities was objectively rational. My answer to the objection, then, is that I am concerned with objective rationality. My argument has been that, in the absence of any reason to suppose that the assignment of the relevant probabilities would be rational, we have no reason to suppose that Pascal's wager would be objectively rational.

## The Value of Belief in God

I have criticized Pascal's wager. But that does not mean that we can say nothing about the value of a belief in God; and here I am particularly interested in the abstract conception of God. Is it, in fact, valuable that one should have such a belief?

---

[2] See Jeff Jordan, 'Pascal's Wager Revisited', *Religious Studies* 34 (1998), 419–32.

## Rewards in an Afterlife

Even if one were not impressed by Pascal's wager, one might still think that the value, or part of the value, of belief in God was constituted by rewards in an afterlife. Now, in fact, as I mentioned at the outset, the core belief which I have been defending does not have anything to say about an afterlife, or about any possible rewards in an afterlife for a believer. But in any case it would, surely, not be reasonable to appeal to any such consideration by itself. For, if there is an afterlife, and those who believe in God will benefit from the fact that they do so, it must surely be because there is something *else* that is good about such a belief, in virtue of which it is *good* that they should benefit from it. Are there any others things that we can point to?

## The Intrinsic Value of Rational Belief

The first and most obvious thing to say is that it is valuable to have rational beliefs about important matters, and especially valuable to have rational true beliefs. And since the question of why this world exists is surely a very important matter, it is a correspondingly good thing that we should have a rational belief about it. And further, if what I believe is true, that the world exists because it is good that it should, it is indeed good if we rationally believe that this is so.

## Gratitude and Worship

On the traditional conception of God we could point to the importance of knowing about our creator, so that we could be grateful to him and worship him. These notions, however, of gratitude and worship do not apply literally in the case of the abstract conception of God, since gratitude and worship are attitudes to persons. But things which are to some degree analogous do. We can recognize the fact that the world is as it is with *gladness*. And that is surely a good thing, to view good things with gladness. Perhaps, indeed, that is not so very much further from the notion of gratitude to God when conceived of as a person, than the notion of gratitude to God, so conceived, is from ordinary gratitude to other people. Again, we can view the power of goodness with humility; we can recognize that its role in the creation of the world is of an order quite different from any role *we* can play in doing good things in the world. And this incorporates something of what is involved in the idea of the worship of God, when God is conceived of as a person. And perhaps it is a good attitude to have.

## Knowledge of Good and Bad

It is commonly thought that we need to know of God's existence in order to know how we ought to act; because to know how we ought to act is to know the will of God. In fact, however, this line of thought is faulty. In so far as we think of God in traditional terms, it is wrong to think of God's will as determining what we should do. It does not determine basic facts about good and bad; or so I argued in Chapter 5. Nor is it plausible to think that it determines what we should do because of some principle that we ought to obey God; or so I argued, in effect, when I discussed the relation between divine commands and duty in Chapter 5. In so far as our conception is the abstract conception, things are a little different. For, on that conception, to know the basic facts about good and bad just *is* to know the will of God. But, nonetheless, it does not follow that to know such things we need to know that God exists. The reason is that we can know the basic facts about good and bad without *thinking* of them as the will of God—in particular, we may have no belief at all about the creative power of goodness. So, on either conception, knowledge of the basic facts about good and bad does not require belief in the existence of God.

However, there is another reason why it may be important to know that the world was created by God. It may be that this fact in itself has a bearing on how we ought to behave. And this may be as true on the abstract view as on the traditional view. And yet, on closer inspection, it is not clear that it is the belief that it was created by God that is the important belief here. The important belief is, rather, that it is good that there should be a world such as this, rather than that it exists for that reason. And we can have the former belief without the latter. I say that it is an important belief, though it is not very easy to say *why* it is important. Part of the reason will be that it is just good to recognize goodness wherever it is to be found. Part of the reason also will be that the belief that the world is inherently good may help us to make good choices. *May* help us. It will not, I take it, tell us that we should or should not be vegetarians; or that we should or should not build a bypass at the expense of wildlife and beautiful countryside. To believe that the world is inherently good is not, of course, to believe that *nothing* should be tampered with in the interests of man; but nor is it to say that any particular thing has value, or has more or less value than something else. Indeed, if anything, that way of thinking would get things the wrong way round. Our primary reason for thinking that the world is inherently good is our belief that this, and this, and this, which it contains or makes possible, are good. Perhaps, though, the belief that the world is inherently good goes beyond any particular recognition of goodness; and perhaps it matters because, even if it does not tell us *what* is good about it, it may make us more sensitive to the possible presence of good, more open to finding it, more likely to appreciate it. And that is surely good: good not only because it may help us to make good choices, and not only because it is good in itself to appreciate goodness, but also because we are likely to be better off, happier, if we do not think of the world as an alien, hostile place. And, in fact, this attitude of looking for goodness may be assisted by the thought that the world exists because it is good. Because that may encourage the thought that there may, for that reason, be more of value to be found than what struck us as good about the world in the first place. But we should not exaggerate the importance either of the thought that the world exists because it is good, or even of the thought that the world is good. It *does* indeed matter that we should be sensitive to the presence of goodness; but this sensitivity surely does not *require* any belief about the goodness of the world.


## Belief in Objective Value

Part of what is involved in a belief in God on the abstract conception is a belief in objective value. But, of course, one could quite well believe in this without believing in God. Is it, though, at least very important to have this belief in objective value, even in the absence of any belief in God? (Assuming, of course, that objective value exists.) Well, it is, no doubt, worth having a correct belief about an important metaphysical issue. But what more can be said? One might be tempted to say that the recognition of objective value was necessary in order to recognize one's own limitations; *we* do not create good and evil. But someone who does not believe in objective value need not think that we create good and evil; he may, quite soberly, think that there is no such thing as good or evil; just attitudes, desires, choices. One might also be tempted to think that such a person might value the wrong things, or nothing at all; might behave wickedly, or selfishly. And it *may* be true that *some* people, on coming to believe that there is no such thing as objective value, might become selfish, for instance; but it is not obvious *why* this should happen. Certainly it would not suddenly become *rational* to value one's own welfare above that of others; nor need the subjectivist suppose such a thing. On the contrary, he may well think, as Hume did, that rationality has nothing to do with preferences at all. And a person may care just as passionately about the welfare of others, whether or not he believes in the objective rightness of it; somewhat as a person may be passionate about the fortunes of a football club, without thinking that it is objectively right that his club should win. And, for what it is worth, those philosophers who do not believe in objective value seem to be every bit as morally good as those who do. However, the question of the actual consequences of not believing in objective value is, of course, one which I am not competent to answer.

## Conclusion

I have argued that it is rational to believe in God, conceived of in a certain way. This conception, I have argued, does justice both to our ideas about goodness and to the idea that God is sovereign. At the same time, even though it does not represent God as a person, it allows us to attribute to him properties which form the key elements in many people's conception of God. The belief in such a God, I have argued, is no more than a natural extension of our ordinary ways of thinking: of our belief in objective value and our scientific outlook. It is a belief, in particular, which does not commit us to the existence of any entities to which we are not already committed by these ordinary ways of thinking.

I have also argued that it is good to have this belief in God. But, however good it may be to have this belief, there is something which is, I think, of greater importance; something which in itself requires neither philosophy, nor theology, nor even religion. I mean *knowledge of God's will*. For to know God's will just is to know what is good and what is bad. And nothing is more important than that.

# BIBLIOGRAPHY

ADAMS, ROBERT M. 'Divine Command Metaethics Modified Again', in his *The Virtue of Faith* (Oxford: Oxford University Press, 1987); first published in *The Journal of Religious Ethics* 7 (1979), 66–79.

—— 'A Modified Divine Command Theory of Ethical Wrongness', in his *The Virtue of Faith* (Oxford: Oxford University Press, 1987); first published in Gene Outka and John P. Reeder (eds.), *Religion and Morality* (Garden City, N.Y.: Anchor, 1973).

—— 'Must God Create the Best?', in his *The Virtue of Faith* (Oxford: Oxford University Press, 1987); first published in *Philosophical Review* 81 (1972), 317–32.

ALSTON, WILLIAM P. 'Christian Experience and Christian Belief', in Alvin Plantinga and Nicholas Wolterstoff (eds.), *Faith and Rationality* (Notre Dame, Ind.: University of Notre Dame Press, 1986).

—— 'Functionalism and Theological Language', in his *Divine Nature and Human Language* (Ithaca, N.Y.: Cornell University Press, 1989), first published in *American Philosophical Quarterly* 22 (1985), 221–30.

—— *Perceiving God* (Ithaca, N.Y.: Cornell University Press, 1991).

—— 'Some Suggestions for Divine Command Theorists', in his *Divine Nature and Human Language* (Ithaca, N.Y.: Cornell University Press, 1989); first published in Michael Beaty (ed.), *Christian Theism and the Problems of Philosophy* (Notre Dame, Ind.: University of Notre Dame Press, 1989).

AYER, A. J. *Language, Truth and Logic*, 2nd edn. (London: Gollancz, 1947).

BLACKBURN, SIMON. *Spreading the Word* (Oxford: Clarendon Press, 1984).

BONJOUR, LAURENCE. *In Defence of Pure Reason* (Cambridge: Cambridge University Press, 1998).

—— *The Structure of Empirical Knowledge* (Cambridge, Mass.: Harvard University Press, 1985).

DAVIDSON, DONALD. 'Actions, Reasons and Causes', in his *Essays on Actions and Events* (Oxford: Clarendon Press, 1980); first published in *Journal of Philosophy* 60 (1963), 685–700.

—— 'Radical Interpretation', in his *Inquiries into Truth and Interpretation*

(Oxford: Clarendon Press, 1984); first published in *Dialectica* 27 (1973), 313–28.

DESCARTES, R. Letter to Mesland, 2 May 1644, in *The Philosophical Writings of Descartes*, vol. iii, trans. J. Cottingham, R. Stoothoff, D. Murdoch, and A. Kenny (Cambridge: Cambridge University Press, 1991), 235 (AT IV 118–19).

—— *Meditations on First Philosophy* (first published 1641), in *The Philosophical Writings of Descartes*, vol. ii, trans. J. Cottingham, R. Stoothoff, and D. Murdoch (Cambridge: Cambridge University Press, 1984).

EWING, A. C. 'Two "Proofs" of God's Existence', *Religious Studies* 1 (1966), 29–46.

GOODMAN, NELSON. *Fact, Fiction and Forecast* (Cambridge, Mass.: Harvard University Press, 1955).

HARE, R. M. *Freedom and Reason* (Oxford: Clarendon Press, 1963).

HARMAN, G. 'The Inference to the Best Explanation', *Philosophical Review* 74 (1965), 88–95.

HASKER, WILLIAM. *God, Time and Knowledge* (Ithaca, N.Y.: Cornell University Press, 1989).

HERBERT, GEORGE. *The Elixir*, from *The Works of George Herbert*, ed. F. E. Hutchinson (Oxford: Clarendon Press, 1941), 184.

HICK, JOHN. *Evil and the God of Love*, 2nd edn. (London: Macmillan, 1977).

HUME, DAVID. *Dialogues Concerning Natural Religion* (first published 1779), ed. R. H. Popkin (Indianapolis, Ind.: Hackett, 1980).

—— *An Enquiry concerning Human Understanding* (first published 1748), ed. L. A. Selby-Bigge, 2nd edn. (Oxford: Clarendon Press, 1902).

—— *A Treatise of Human Nature* (first published 1739), ed. L. A. Selby-Bigge (Oxford: Clarendon Press, 1888).

JORDAN, JEFF. 'Pascal's Wager Revisited', *Religious Studies* 34 (1998), 419–32.

LESLIE, JOHN. *Value and Existence* (Oxford: Blackwell, 1979).

McDOWELL, J. 'Are Moral Requirements Hypothetical Imperatives?', *Proceedings of the Aristotelian Society*, supp. vol. 52 (1978), 13–29.

MACKIE, J. L. *The Cement of the Universe: A Study of Causation* (Oxford: Clarendon Press, 1974).

—— *Ethics: Inventing Right and Wrong* (Harmondsworth: Penguin, 1977).

—— *The Miracle of Theism* (Oxford: Clarendon Press, 1982).

MOLINA, LUIS DE. *On Divine Foreknowledge (Part IV of the Concordia)*, trans. Alfred J. Freddoso (Ithaca, N.Y.: Cornell University Press, 1988).

PASCAL, BLAISE. *Pensées*, trans. Honor Levi (Oxford: Oxford University Press, 1999).

## Bibliography

PLANTINGA, ALVIN. *The Nature of Necessity* (Oxford: Clarendon Press, 1974).

—— 'Reason and Belief in God', in Alvin Plantinga and Nicholas Wolterstoff (eds.), *Faith and Rationality* (Notre Dame, Ind.: University of Notre Dame Press, 1986).

QUINE, W. V. 'Truth by Convention', in his *The Ways of Paradox* (Cambridge, Mass.: Harvard University Press, 1976).

SELLARS, WILFRID. 'Empiricism and the Philosophy of Mind', in his *Science, Perception and Reality* (London: Routledge & Kegan Paul, 1963).

SWINBURNE, RICHARD. *The Christian God* (Oxford: Clarendon Press, 1994).

—— *The Coherence of Theism* (Oxford: Clarendon Press, 1977).

—— *The Existence of God* (Oxford: Clarendon Press, 1979).

—— *Providence and the Problem of Evil* (Oxford: Clarendon Press, 1998).

WALKER, RALPH C. S. *The Coherence Theory of Truth* (London: Routledge, 1989).

—— *Kant* (London: Routledge, 1978).

WOLTERSTOFF, NICHOLAS. 'Can Belief in God be Rational if it Has No Foundations?', in Alvin Plantinga and Nicholas Wolterstoff (eds.), *Faith and Rationality* (Notre Dame, Ind.: University of Notre Dame Press, 1986).

—— *Divine Discourse: Philosophical Reflections on the Claim that God Speaks* (New York, N.Y.: Cambridge University Press, 1995).

# INDEX

a priori beliefs 32–3, 37–47
abstract conception of God, *see* God,
  abstract conception
Adams, Robert M. 68 n, 70 n, 109 n
afterlife, *see* life after death
Alston, William P. 66 nn, 89 n, 125 n
animal suffering, *see* evil, the problem
  of
authority, deference to 125–7
Ayer, A. J. 18 n

belief in God 5, 48, 50, 89
  value of 5, 134–9
  importance of rationality 5, 128–34
  rationality of 1, 2
  uninferred 125–7
Blackburn, Simon 19 nn, 41 n
BonJour, Laurence 38 n, 46 n, 126 n

causation 52–9, 95
coherence and reasonable beliefs 31,
  126–7
coherence theory of truth 40–1
concepts 9, 55–6, 61–3
creation 4, 50–2, 54

Darwinian accounts
  of beliefs in necessary truths 42–4
  of moral beliefs 27, 33–4, 35–6
  of scientific procedures 61–3
Davidson, Donald 23 n, 95 n
Descartes, R. 39, 45 n, 69 n, 91 n
divine command theory of ethics 67,
  82–7
divine will theory of ethics 67–72
duty 82–7

emotivist theories of ethics 18
empiricist picture 7–9, 10, 12, 13, 14, 28

epistemic oddity, *see* objective value
epistemic security 7–8, 13, 14
evil, the problem of 4, 90–114
  appeals to ignorance 91–2
  free will defence 93–102, 111
  the good of knowledge 105–7
  gratuitous evil 110–11
  no good without evil 92–3
  soul-making 107–9
  terrible lives 111–14
  unintended evils 101–5, 110–11
  whether God must create the best
    109–11
Ewing, A. C. 49 n
existence of the world, *see* goodness, as
  explanation of the existence of the
  world
explanation
  belief in 2, 15
  and laws 52–9
  stopping points 59–60

free will 93–101, 111

given 7–9
God
  abstract conception 72–89, 109, 114,
    127, 134–9
  action 72–6, 88–9; *see also* miracles
  commands 81–7
  creator 72–3, 89, 135–8
  feelings 77
  giving information 8–9
  his knowledge 76, 88–9, 96–101
  his love 77, 112–13, 124–5
  mediating 3, 50–2, 53, 54, 63, 64, 65,
    88–9
  and morality 64–72, 82–7
  omnipotence 90–1, 99 n, 101
  omniscience 76, 90–1

God (*cont.*)
  as person 88–9
  promises 79–81
  role in the world 127
  sovereignty 64–7
  speech 78
  his will and goodness 4, 67–76, 88–9
  *see also* belief in God; knowledge of
    God
Goodman, Nelson 9 n
goodness
  basic facts about, *see* value, basic
    facts about
  causal efficacy 3, 51; *see also* neces-
    sary facts, causal efficacy
  as explanation of the existence of the
    world 3, 48–63
  and God's will, *see* God, his will and
    goodness
  rationality of belief in 3
  reliability of belief in 3
  *see also* objective value
gratitude to God 135–6

Hare, R. M. 21 n
Harman 15 n
Hasker, William 98 n
Herbert, George 50 n
Hick, John 107 n
Hume, David 10–11, 13, 14, 16, 18, 21,
    52 n, 55 n, 90 n, 95 n, 116 n, 138
Humean view of ethics 16–23

intelligibility 15, 48, 63, 103, 107

Jordan, Jeff 134 n

knowledge of God and knowledge of
    and good and bad 136–8, 139

laws of nature
  belief in 10–11
  explanation of 49, 53–4
  *see also* miracles
Leibniz, G. W. 45 n
Leslie, John 49 n
life after death, belief in 5, 135
logical truths 25, 28–9; *see also* neces-
    sary truths

McDowell, J. 21 n
Mackie, J. L. 23 n, 56 nn, 82 n, 92 n,
    97 n, 117 n
metaphysical hygiene 7–8
metaphysical necessity 30; *see also*
    necessary truths
metaphysical oddity, *see* objective value
middle knowledge 96–101
miracles 4, 115–27
  need of 122–5
  reasons for belief in 118–25
  uninferred belief in 125–7
  and violations of laws of nature
    115–17
Molina, Luis de 97 n

necessary facts, causal efficacy 38, 46–7
necessary truths 29–31, 37–47
  reasonableness of belief in 3, 38–47

objective value 16–36
  belief in 2, 3, 16–23
  causal efficacy 3, 48, 51; *see also*
    necessary facts, causal efficacy
  disagreements 16, 23, 27–8, 33–4,
    35–6
  epistemic oddity 23, 26–7, 31–3
  existence of 23–36
  metaphysical oddity 23, 24–6, 28–31,
    35
omnipotence 90–1, 99 n, 101
omniscience 76, 90–1
order
  belief in 2, 3, 11
  and objective value 48–50
  *see also* goodness, as explanation of
    the existence of the world

Pascal's wager 132–4
Plantinga, Alvin 93 n, 100 n, 125 n
pre-established harmony 45–6, 63

Quine, W. V. 29 n

rationality, belief in 2, 11–14, 29
reliability and reasonable belief 38–40
religious belief, *see* belief in God

Schrödinger's cat 57–8

scientific outlook 1–2, 7–15
scientific procedures, rationality of
    61–3; *see also* support by evidence
Sellars, Wilfrid 9 n
support by evidence 12–14, 22, 29–30, 34
    basic facts about 30
Swinburne, Richard 53 n, 57 n, 65 n,
    70 n, 83 n, 93 n, 105 n, 113 n

trust, the value of 131–2

uninferred beliefs, reasonableness of
    125–7

value
    basic facts about 24–36
    necessity of basic facts about 30–1,
      69, 72
    *see also* objective value

Walker, Ralph C. S. 9 n, 45 n, 61 n
Wolterstoff, Nicholas 78 n, 125 n
world, existence of, *see* goodness, as
    explanation of the existence of the
    world
worship 135–6